A View from the Fields

A View from the Fields

Calvin Miller

Broadman Press
Nashville, Tennessee

4255–20
ISBN: 0–8054–5520–5

Unless otherwise noted, all Scripture quotations are taken from the King James Version of the Bible. Scripture quotations marked TLB are taken from *The Living Bible.* Copyright © Tyndale House Publishers, Wheaton, Illinois, 1971. Used by permission.

Dewey Decimal Classification: 269
Subject headings: EVANGELISTIC WORK//CHURCH GROWTH

Library of Congress Catalog Card Number: 78–062399
Printed in the United States of America

Acknowledgments

I have forgotten the individual moments that comprised the past sixteen years. I can pinpoint large events, for I recorded the milestones. Since the events are more relevant to me than to you, I will not retrace that road. It is not necessary for you to know that I have started two churches or that the second has been my pastorate for the past eleven years.

It is important to me that you know I was befriended by a superb group in Atlanta, Georgia. The materials in this book were developed at their request for presentation at colloquiums, clinics, retreats, and conferences.

But I owe them much more. In moments of insecurity, I took refuge in their support. With their help and with the empowering of the Holy Spirit, I have been able to grow a church in Omaha. From eighteen members in 1966, membership has grown to around eight hundred. Two or three people per week have joined the church for more than ten years. Too much credit for the growth has come to me, so I wish to pass on some deserved praise to the Church Extension Department of the Home Mission Board.

I offer my special thanks to:

Dr. Wendell Belew, who has been my mentor and inspiration. He taught me the priority of evangelism in missions, offered me friendship, and encouraged me to be creative in doing God's thing.

Quentin Lockwood, who helped me deal with my fears of a city ministry. His encouragement prefaced a decade of joy.

Jack Redford, whose tough-minded optimism kept me easy in the frenzy. Jack constantly invited me to participate in programs where I felt a need to argue cogently for church growth, thus precipitating the material in this book.

And of course *my wife, Barbara,* whose support is most important to me. Her work on this manuscript was essential. Even more essential has been her buoyant encouragement from year to year.

Preface

A View from the Fields

Church growth as a term is phenomenal to this decade. And yet in practice, growth is a basic New Testament view. Mark recorded the parable of the mustard seed. The maturation of the tiny seed to a giant tree is explicitly referring to church growth. The growth this parable illustrates is numerical. Many are opposed to the idea of mathematics in the Kingdom. For them the categories of "better Christians" and "more Christians" are antithetical. But I know of no way to grow a *deeper* church without growing a *bigger* church.

After Elmer Towns published *The Ten Largest Sunday Schools In America,* he was asked to write a book on small dynamic Sunday Schools. After some research he concluded that the "small dynamic" church does not exist. If a church is dynamic, it does not remain small. Conversely, if it remains small, it lacks dynamics. Growth, then, is the validation of the church. Every great church is not a big church, but every great church is a growing church.

It was never my goal to grow a church—or, for that matter, to write a book on the subject. I hasten to say that it would have done me little good to try. The building of the church is the task of Christ and his Spirit. I see the true beginning of the church in Luke 24:49: "And behold, I send the promise of my Father upon you: but tarry ye in the city of Jerusalem until ye be endued with power from on high." I think a good paraphrase of this verse would be: "Don't do anything till you hear from God."

The basic principle for growing a church is obedience to the Spirit. This command to tarry was not permission to take it easy for a few days. Rather, it was an assignment of the most demanding work of all—praying and searching through the Spirit for the will and power of God.

In Acts 2, the church erupted in joy. Thousands came to Christ at one invitation. But Peter and the witnesses were not trying to grow a church—they were trying to be obedient. They defined obedience in terms of rescue work! The world was lost in sin. Only two and one-half months before the empowering of the church, men crucified the "only begotten of the Father, full of grace and truth" (John 1:14).

In the upper room they waited upon the Spirit in patient prayer. James did not approach Peter and say, "Look, Peter, here is a book that says if we're going to make this work, we have to think in terms of 'cross-cultural' growth. We can't be too cautious concerning our 'survival goal index.'" (To which Peter would have replied, "Huh?") They had to begin without even sampling their community. Without a single volume on church growth, they launched out in the urgency of their mission.

When I began my work in Omaha, I assumed that because Jesus was in rescue work, I should be also. Thus, on a summer afternoon nearly eleven years ago, I walked the streets with a shirt pocket full of Bill Bright booklets. I was hungry to liberate the captives, but I couldn't seem to find them. There were 600,000 people in Omaha, none of whom I knew. There were multitudes of handbooks and techniques, but I wanted the direction of the Spirit.

So I petitioned the Home Mission Board, asked for five student helpers, and began an analysis of our community. In eight weeks we surveyed almost five thousand homes. To our amazement, 64 percent of the families were Catholic; 20 percent were Lutheran; and 6 percent were Jewish.

Occasionally we would meet a Baptist and fill out the historic survey card. But the Baptists were rarely Southern Baptists. They were Independent, Northern, American, North American, North American Swedish, or Independent North American Swedish, etc. Only one-half of 1 percent were Southern Baptist!

I could tell this would not be an easy place to try to build a Southern Baptist church. I was very discouraged and might have thrown the whole affair overboard. Fortunately, I believed that I was called to do rescue work.

Survival in my nonevangelical world became an issue. I do not champion my own suffrage. Life for many pastors in the newer areas of our Convention is arduous. When the task is overwhelming, only obedience provides the courage to stay.

Things have become easier for me in the intervening years. My ministry has been a source of joy. It is all of Christ and none of me. The times I have tried to steer my own course I have made shipwreck of my circumstances.

Because Christ is the bedrock of every spiritual venture, I wanted to set it out here at the first of the book, lest anyone presume that there is a cheaper way to grow a church in any area of the Convention.

Admittedly, the sermons and papers that follow this foreword lack the scholarly sound of certain popular monographs on church growth. Their virtue is that their origin was brewed in the caldron of experience. The Savior once called his evangelistic reapers to harvest the fields "white already to harvest" (John 4:35). There have been scores of books written to call the harvest hands from the seminaries to the fields. The books are often the most noble offerings that the theoretician can offer.

The view from the lectern too often produces a remote harvest. Perhaps it is really in behalf of all my fellow strugglers in the newer areas of the Convention that I wish to offer this view from the fields.

CALVIN MILLER

Omaha, Nebraska

Contents

Spiritual Awareness and Church Growth

1
Growing in the Spirit of Renewal

(Numbers 11:24–29; Acts 2:1–4)

The growing church is empowered by the spirit of renewal. A renewed church is described as *independent, intrepid, intriguing.* To such a church the Holy Spirit is characterized by those same adjectives. Any attempt to renew the church without involving the Holy Spirit would be disastrous, for he alone provides the catalyst for renewal.

The evangelical church that is not growing demonstrates this principle clearly. The cleverest contrivances are unavailing. We season our sermons with doctrinal clichés, but renewal does not come. We nibble the tastiest hors d'ouevres of institutional pedagogy, but the main course never follows. We read hungrily through the manuals, while spontaneity evades us. We say, "Keep trying." Renewal is just beyond our present dyspepsia— hidden behind the next quarrel. "It will come like a lightning in the east with the next conventional revelation," we promise our hungry congregations. It does not.

The fire of renewal was lit at Pentecost, We still say what Simon Peter did, but the fisherman's fire blazed brighter than our anemic flame.

Last Christmas one of our members gave my family a Yule candle. The square taper read vertically, "*Noel.*" The message glowed beneath the light. The burning flame, however, altered the message. When the candle had burned a fourth of its length, only the letters "*o-e-l*" remained. Then "*e-l.*" Then "*l.*" Then nothing. The living flame consumed the message.

We often behave as though we believe that the Spirit flame

is bent on a similar consumption of our message. The converse is true: mechanically contrived messages are more often a threat to the flame. We think we must huddle around the Spirit fire and keep it warm. We view ourselves as his preserver and keeper. But we cannot sustain such fire; nor can we originate it.

The Spirit's fire will burn only in the man or church bent to his purpose. Witness Eldad and Medad in Numbers 11. Moses and the seventy elders were visited by the Spirit, began prophesying, and wouldn't quit. Eldad and Medad were "eight-to-five" laymen who wouldn't have had time to attend the all-day evangelism conference, even if they had been invited. Suddenly the Spirit caught Eldad and Medad and they began prophesying too. First Eldad preached and Medad said "Amen"—then Medad preached and Eldad said "Amen." Soon the whole camp was gathered around them.

It was embarrassing. Moses and the elders were having a wonderful time. The smoke and fire of empowered preaching was theirs. Then came the word "There's revival in the camp!" At first they were amused. Who would try a revival during convention week? A motion was made by Joshua, the son of Nun, to silence Eldad and Medad until they could be ordained and measured for robes. At this point Moses said: "Would God that all the Lord's people were prophets, and that the Lord would put his spirit upon them" (Num. 11:29).

Renewal cannot come to your church until you are willing to say with Moses, "I wish all the Lord's people were prophets and that he would put his hand upon them." Renewal must be a people's movement.

1. Independent

I need to preface my next remarks with a loyalty oath. I am a Southern Baptist—a member of and the pastor of a Southern Baptist church. I am committed to Southern Baptist teachings and programs. I believe that it is possible to have a renewed church within the Southern Baptist structure. But I do not believe that renewal can come *from the structure.* If it comes, as in the case of Eldad and Medad, it will come from the Spirit. This is not to say that the Spirit must operate independently of the structure, for in most instances they are mutually beneficent. But "the wind bloweth where it listeth, and thou . . . canst not tell whence it cometh, and whither it goeth" (John 3:8).

William Golding indicted us in *The Spire.* His novel tells of a priest with a compulsion to add a four-hundred-foot tower and spire to his cathedral. Father Jocelin is advised against building the ill-fated tower. He presses on, however. The builder, Roger Mason, digs in vain for a gravel base on which to lay the foundation stones. The digging disturbs graves in the cathedral floor, releasing all sorts of foul odors, especially during the rainy season. When the pit is already too deep and no gravel has yet appeared, the tower construction is begun anyway.

On its unsure foundation the tower is doomed. The stone columns sing in the agony of trying to hold the tower steady while resting on a spongy foundation.

Fearful communicants cease coming, and finally the great church is empty. Even the swallows leave their nests in the stone arches. The cathedral, though beautiful, is unsafe. The structure prevented worship within.

The symbolism is obvious. Structure can threaten renewal and the Holy Spirit. The Holy Spirit loves spontaneity, freedom, creativity, and openness. He is threatened by rigidity, tradition, and intricate programming. Too often we ask the Holy Spirit to "Come in freedom and power—but leave the machinery intact."

Unwilling to disturb our cybernetics, we force the Spirit of God to do most of his work outside the constitution. So we had Eldad and Medad preaching in the camp. We had Wesley and St. Francis in the fields. We had General Booth on the slum sidewalks. Even Christ was evicted from the Nazarene synagogue.

Since the Spirit is independent of the structure, we must make sure he has landing room when he arrives. We must give him time for his work, and we must give him space. We must pray that his presence hallow the people more than the programs. He will not work otherwise.

Further, we must extend to everyone the right to be Spirit-possessed. Most pastors mentally preclude most of their people as capable of renewal. They say with Joshua to Eldad and Medad, "You boys just remember that your job is to fold and pack sections 37 to 53 of the tabernacle, and God help you if we catch you preaching." If the Holy Spirit really came to our churches, we would be aghast to discover which members are capable of infilling (those we felt were alien to even the suggestion).

To bring renewal you must offer the Spirit your people without reserve. You must give him the freedom to tamper with them in any way he wishes. Every life he touches will be fired with God's redemptive program. In some places that may match the program you have established already; in some places it may not. I pray that where there are conflicts between your program and God's program, you might have wisdom to choose. We must be willing to grant independence to him. We must give him room to work, for he is the Great Independent. When the Spirit comes, there is renewal. When true renewal comes, church growth is the natural corollary.

2. Intrepid

Japan, the leader in transistorized radios and cameras, now manufactures a laugh box. When you push a button on the box, a recording plays laughter. Once activated by the button, the laugh cycle is impossible to stop. It plays through the whole sequence before shutting off.

I was unaware that such a laugh box existed until recently. At a hospital I stepped into an elevator full of people. I leaped into the crowd and flattened myself into the press. In the process, I accidentally triggered the laugh box a man was carrying to his son. My elbow must have bumped the button, for suddenly laughter began. I looked at the man and his face turned red. I wanted to apologize for making his box laugh, but the idea seemed absurd. He managed to stick the box under his overcoat. On and on it laughed.

As nothing is as infectious as laughter, I began laughing too. Then the other passengers began laughing. But the little box outdid us all. It would not be shushed.

The Spirit of God is like that. He cannot be turned on and off at will. Once he settles on a man or congregation, he is there. Eldad and Medad would not be silent, even when asked. Spirit force cannot be shushed.

In Acts 4 Annas, Caiaphas, Alexander, and John commanded Peter and John "not to speak at all nor teach in the name of Jesus." But the intrepid Spirit sent Peter and John back into the marketplace, and they preached Christ everywhere. The man born blind became the man born stubborn under the Spirit's influence. He gave witness to Jesus under duress of excommunication. The dauntless Spirit, banned in Whitfield's church houses, went to the fields.

It is this intrepidity that causes us to fear him. We're afraid of things we cannot asterisk in bulletins. A street service (see Acts 2) without mimeographed leaflets is horrifying. We don't want anything in our churches that cannot be canceled in case of embarrassment.

But you see, he is the great activist. Acts 2:2 says, "It filled all the house where they were sitting." They were motionless. *He* moved. They sat. *He* surged. They moved silently into the streets. *He* set their tongues ablaze. Their Aramaic grammar faded and was born again in a hundred different languages. But it was not they. It was him—the Intrepid Spirit!

To sincerely ask for his fire begs a consuming flame. He may suggest arson for mechanisms we have shielded for decades. He might propose a radical organ transplant (exchange the 32-

pedal, 3-manual Bach player for something that personally interprets "I will sing the wondrous story of the Christ who died for me"). He might invite the softball team to visitation on Thursday night.

Only the brave can sing "Holy Spirit, Breathe on Me" with meaning. Fearful people realize that they don't want him breathing down their necks. To the person in the comfortable pew the Holy Spirit seems more Disturber than Comforter. We sing, "Come Holy Comforter, Thy sacred witness bear" in four parts, but always with tongue in cheek.

The Holy Spirit is the only agent of renewal and church growth, but he cannot be lured partially into service. He must come in toto or not at all. It is futile to entice him into worship and try to close him out of business. We must invite him *all the way* into our fellowship, surrendering to his creative management.

3. Intriguing

In Numbers 11:26, the Spirit rested upon Eldad and Medad and they stayed in camp and preached. Why did their words draw such a crowd? The Spirit was upon them and wove about them a mystery. His intrigue captivated the people! The hallmark of the Holy Spirit is mystery and intrigue. His mystery lures people to investigate him, and when they do they are caught.

Now people come into our cut-and-dried services and say, "What happened to the mystery? Where is the intrigue?" We explain everything from the Genesis myths to the church budget. We vivisect doctrines and expose miracles. We console irresponsibly like Kierkegaard's priest, and when the weeping pentitents come we counsel as did he: "Do not cry, poor brother, the whole thing might be a lie." [1] We tamper with the intrigue and the mystery is gone.

Christianity came alive in the first century in a "What's Next" context:

I won a charioteer while a hitchhiker! What's next!

I healed a cripple and he ran at the temple gate. What's next!

I preached, I did it. Me! I preached. I can't preach, but I preached. Three thousand were saved! What's next!

I raised the dead. What's next!

When I ask "What's next?" I get such answers as "the Sweetheart Banquet" or "the Forward Program." Nobody has to guess what's next: We keep it mimeographed one year ahead. There is nothing inscrutable about us. Nothing unpredictable. Nothing mysterious. Worship and practice seem always the same.

The great questions of the faith are unanswerable. The Holy Spirit was not sent to take the interrogatives out of the kingdom of God. On the contrary, he was sent to create a womb of intrigue. We need to pray: "Lord, send back the Divine Mystery. We don't need understanding; we need renewal. Infill, confront our reason, and change our lives. Come, Holy Spirit, so we may breathe your presence and grow so great a church that the gates of hell may yield to us."

Note

1. Soren Kierkegaard, *Attack Upon Christendom* (Boston: Moody Press, 1956), p. 181.

2
Examining the Various Models of Church Growth

The Holy Spirit is best able to use those who are in touch with themselves. Churches suffer from "sameness syndrome." Because one man grows a dynamic fellowship with Sunday School buses, we assume that buses must be the will of God for all churches.

From such assumptions proceed the "fads" of church growth: WIN clinics, puppet shows, Backyard Bible Clubs, Sunday School enlargement campaigns. The best strategy for church growth does not lie in xeroxing other programs, but in observing the methods of those churches that are growing and applying their best principles to our own situations. There is no end to the possible models for growing churches. But the key to applying someone else's techniques lies in being sure that we not only correctly assess our ability to use them successfully but also that we are sure their programs are transferable to our own fellowship.

Further, it is always a good idea to be sure that we have used our own unique gifts before we adopt someone else's. We must remember that God puts within every life unique gifts. Some who could do an authentic and beautiful work bypass their own authenticity pursuing someone else's.

Many end up like the little boy always running to that section of the stream where the fish seem more abundant. Barely does the lad dangle his hook than someone hauls the catch from another section, and he is off again. He could become a fisherman in his own right, but he is too busy padding the bank for "hot spots."

The world will walk a long way to see a new thing. So what lies within our own lives should be the first place we pursue the richness of God's blessing. We should fish the deep waters of our own existence for a rare offering of something to offer unto God that will indeed make our churches grow. Individuality is a powerful and genuine treasure, and we must not neglect its richness in seeking to build his church.

But we can learn from others. Dan Baumann, who leads the Whittier Area Baptist Fellowship, has posed the legitimate question in his book and lecture series: *All Originality Makes a Dull Church*. It is his view that "stealing" may be "sanctified" at times. What we may legitimately put to work from someone else's experience ought to be used. His book title is a takeoff on Spurgeon's famous proposition that "all originality and no plagiarism makes a dull sermon." Baumann sees Spirit-driven methods as a collection of all believers for God's use. According to his view, what is instrumental in growing the Kingdom lies beyond copyright. Wherever profitable it should be used to make God's kingdom grow.

As one who has fought for the principle of original expressions rather than the borrowed concept, I want to react to this. Still, I believe that there is a great deal to be learned by examining the work of someone else and by taking shortcuts around their mistakes.

He suggests the models for emulation in a great deal more detail than I would like to do. Further, I would like to put at the top of my list the First Baptist Church of Dallas, Texas, as an example of a church growing by the more traditional denominational programs and emphases. Let us begin there:

1. The First Baptist Church of Dallas, Texas, began prior to the turn of the century, which will not give it quite the recent and contemporary ring of the other models. It was founded some fifty years after Dallas itself was founded on the banks of the Trinity River in 1840. The church grew under the dynamic leadership of George Truett and W. A. Criswell to its present five-digit membership. It is the most denominational of all the

churches and loyal in every sense. It has all the organizations typical to Southern Baptist life and has made good use of them. Since most of the readers of this book are probably enmeshed in that denomination and its programs, it will not be necessary to explain them in any detail.

While Southern Baptists fared especially well during the forties, fifties, and sixties on the ecclesiastical model furnished by such churches as First Baptist Church of Dallas, more and more our new churches are making their own way with deviations from the denominational norm. This is vital to the denomination in its missionary strategy to plant new churches in areas where our denomination is not understood, nor its programs geared to work well in cultures unfriendly to its custom.

Interestingly, many of our mission pastors who began working in the non-Convention areas went to those areas with this model predominant. They offered exactly the same organizations and programs that they had offered in the older, established areas of the Southern Baptist Convention. In some places they appeared to work well; in other areas the growth was slow because the programs may not have fitted the specific need or understanding of the people to whom we felt compelled to present the gospel.

2.   The Thomas Road Baptist Church in Lynchburg, Virginia, is the decade's outstanding study of what has happened in lesser degrees in many Bible Baptist Fellowship churches around the country. Thomas Road is atypical in the furthest aspects of its outreach ministry through promotion and television. But it is a good example of bus ministry and its effect as a church. Since its inception, Thomas Road has grown to fifteen thousand members pastored by a local boy made good. Like so many other pastors of great churches, Jerry Falwell is a workaholic who never takes a vacation, has no hobbies but his church, and sets his hopes for church growth on 125 old, reconditioned buses and the swankiest Madison Avenue promotion techniques. The result is that his is the largest of the thirty-eight Baptist churches in Lynchburg and rapidly becoming one of the largest in the nation.

3. The Coral Ridge Presbyterian Church of Fort Lauderdale, Florida, is barely fifteen years old, having recently moved into its new nine-million-dollar facility. Its six thousand members numbered less than forty originally until its famed "Evangelism Explosion" began to rock its community with a blitz of soul-winners whose weekly attendance at the church now numbers over three hundred adults. James Kennedy, the pastor, believes that this strategic group of three hundred Presbyterians have been responsible for making the Coral Ridge Church the fastest-growing Presbyterian church in America.

The church itself has none of the usual trappings of "soul-winning" churches. It does not have altar calls or baptism by immersion. In this sense, I believe that Kennedy's "Evangelism Explosion" method falls on hard ground in those churches which (like my own) do require a "public profession of faith and baptism" as a prelude to church membership. Kennedy in his training film teaches five principles that lie behind the church evangelism program: First, the church is a body under orders from Christ to evangelize the world. Secondly, he believes that laymen need to be trained to do it. Third, Kennedy believes that ministers should see themselves as coaches to train laymen to do the work of this ministry. Fourth, he believes that evangelism is more "caught" than "taught." And finally, he believes that it is more important to train a soul-winner than it is to win a soul.

4. The Peninsula Bible Church in Palo Alto, California, would be an example of a "classroom" church. This kind of church has been championed mostly, it seems, by various professors and preachers from Dallas Theological Seminary. Palo Alto is in the San Francisco area and is a university town, whose average household averages only 2.4 people and whose entire census is youthful, most likely due to the fact that there are three colleges in the area with a combined enrollment of 34,000 students in a town having only a 53,000 population.

The Peninsula Bible Church is best known for its concept of "Body Life" services where between 1,500 and 2,000 people attend every Sunday night. But the Sunday morning services are even larger and take the classroom approach. Pastor Steadman, after simple hymn singing and a choir or musical special, preaches a forty- to forty-five-minute sermon. It is almost seminary in its scriptural thoroughness. Biblical exegesis is the main diet of the congregation, and the preaching of the biblical truth is the most important thing that occurs in the fellowship.

5.   The House Church Principle of church growth is innovative, new, and best represented by Fellowship Bible Church in North Dallas, pastored by Gene Goetz. They have a Friday night service and three Sunday services attended by all of the "house church" groups that meet together during the week. The one thousand-plus people who attend this church do not see Dr. Goetz as their primary pastor but the elders who lead them in the small unit worships during the week. These elders are ordained and perform marriages and funerals. Dr. Goetz sees ordination not as a speciality of education or denominational endorsement, but as the confirmation of spiritual gifts by the congregation and the Holy Spirit of God.

At the central meeting where all of the house churches come together, Dr. Goetz preaches much along the classroom church model—except that they have a church project each week, to which every one is assigned as well as a special time of refreshment and fellowship when they come together.

6.   Probably not much needs to be said about the Garden Grove Community Church or their popular pastor, Robert Harold Schuller. Schuller says that when he went to Southern California (Orange County) to start his church, there were only four people from his denomination (Reformed Church) that he could find. Two wanted him to start a church; two did not. Undaunted, he surged ahead. On a March morning in 1955 he mounted a concession stand at the Orange Drive-in Theater and began the church with seventy-five people and fifty-one cars. Of the seventy-five people, forty were participants in a choir he had borrowed for the occasion.

Now he has an annual budget of 1.5 million dollars and a soon-to-be-erected Crystal Cathedral. He has grown a church not by scriptural exegesis but by preaching popular psychology and textual sermons that help people to understand themselves and relate to their world. His how-to approach has been punctuated by slogans and clichés, but it is now the most popular preaching program in four of the United States' largest cities.

7.   Charles Swindoll is pastor of another of the classroom churches, but Swindoll has combined with his classroom approach a more typical suburban church program. I have thus added his church (as Dan Baumann does) because in most ways it seems to be a combination of the classroom and suburban program church.

But now that we have set out some of the model churches and briefly alluded to their program and uniqueness, let's go on to ask ourselves some of the vital questions about how much of their program is transferable. Obviously, if you try to take any of the churches in metropolitan Texas or California and apply their methods to rural Kansas or coastal Maine, the results are probably going to be bad. But let us use these churches as springboards to better understand and promote our specific cases of church growth. Complete the graph on the next page by filling in the same statistics for your community. When I filled out my own answer to the graph it looked like this:

Westside	Omaha	600,000	408	1–1470	827

But in this simple act of finding out this information I was learning more and more about my community.

Obviously, two things that tell a great deal about a congregation's growth are its worship or "gathering emphasis" and its style of pastoral leadership. You will notice that (in my opinion) all of the pastoral models we are considering tend to be rather

NAME OF MODEL CHURCH	LOCATION	POPULATION OF CITY	NUMBER OF CHURCHES	CHURCH/ POPULATION RATIO	NUMBER OF MEMBERS IN CONGREGATION
First Baptist	Dallas	940,000	1,140	1-825	20,000 plus
Thomas Road	Lynchburg	55,000	107	1-500 churches	15,000 plus
Coral Ridge	Fort Lauderdale	165,000	198	1-833 churches	6,000 plus
Peninsula Bible	Palo Alto	53,000	50	1-1,160	2,800 attendance
Fellowship Bible	Dallas	940,000	1,140	1-825	1,000 attendance
Garden Grove	Garden Grove	123,000	70	1-1750	7,000 plus
First Evangelical	Fullerton	91,000	37	1-2500	14,000 plus (2800 plus in attendance)
Your Church					

authoritarian in their pastoral style of leadership. James Kennedy might be less so than the others, but I suspect that even Dr. Kennedy is very much that sort of leader. I am prone to see him as the most overtly kind and gracious and "soft" of all the leaders I have referred to, but it would be a matter of my own faulty judgment to offer this evaluation. He is obviously a strong yet personable leader.

One other aspect might be mentioned that does not appear in any column. In a recent publication of the *Home Missions* magazine on the subject of church growth, of the top fifteen pastors of fast-growing Southern Baptist Convention churches, all of them were rated as workaholics in making their churches yield the rich statistics of their reputations. A pastor such as Jerry Falwell states it more clearly than all of the others in saying that his church and its growth is not his job only; it is his work and hobby and calling from which he will not be separated even for a vacation. Bob Schuller firmly believes that a man ought to serve one church for all his calling.

While my statistics are not in the same league as those models I propose, I do believe that one of the barriers to church growth is as simple a matter as the tenure of the pastor. If a pastor will agree to stay at one field of service for a good many years, his opportunities of growing a church are infinitely better than the pastor who is moving frequently from field to field. In almost any church with a great growth record, it will be observed that the church had pastors who stayed for a great part if not all of their lifetimes. One can witness this in the First Baptist Church of Dallas. In its centennial growth to 20,000 members, it has had only two pastors.

On the chart on the next page appears a final slot for the evaluation of your church and your style of ministry. My chart read this way:

Westside	Omaha	12 years	Expository	Worship	Authoritarian	Evangelism/Outreach

NAME OF MODEL CHURCH	LOCATION	PASTOR'S TENURE	SERMON STYLE	PRIORITY EMPHASIS OF GATHERING	LEADERSHIP STYLE	KEY VEHICLE IN GROWTH
First Baptist	Dallas	35 years	Expository	Exposition	Authoritarian	Program
Thomas Road	Lynchburg	22 years	Evangelistic	Evangelism	Authoritarian	Promotion
Coral Ridge	Fort Lauderdale	15 years	Topical/Expository	Worship	Authoritarian	Outreach/Evangelism
Peninsula Bible	Palo Alto	28 years	Expository	Study	Authoritarian	Study/Body Life
Fellowship Bible	Dallas	6 years	Teaching	Study/Fellowship	Authoritarian	Study/Fellowship
Garden Grove	Garden Grove	23 years	Topical/Inspiration	Life-Situation Practical Help	Authoritarian	Promotion/Relational Sermons
First Evangelical	Fullerton	6 years	Expository	Teaching	Authoritarian	Appeal to learn
Your Church						

Again, this chart emphasizes the importance of pastoral longevity in growing these churches. In the seven churches listed above, there is a cumulative pastoral tenure of 135 years or an astounding average of 19 years per pastor per church.

So often in the newer areas of Convention work our average has been two and one-half years for the average tenure of a pastor before he moves to some other field. In such rapid shifting from church to church, not much genuine, measurable growth occurs.

On the final schematic there appears a contrast of the nature of the community and the church and its teaching. Once again there is a place for you to fill in these same statistics on your church and your community.

My own church properly related to the following schematic would read:

Westside	1968	Upper middle	Non-Evangeli-cal Jewish Catholic	Every service	Immer-sion	The most emphasized program of the church

Perhaps in studying the various models of some of America's most reputable fast-growing churches, you will be able to devise a program compatible with your talents and adequate for your community.

NAME OF CHURCH	YEAR BEGUN	TYPE OF COMMUNITY	RELIGIOUS CHARACTER OF THE CHURCH COMMUNITY	FREQUENCY OF PUBLIC ALTAR CALL	TYPE OF BAPTISM EMPHASIZED	EXISTENCE OF SOUL-WINNING PROGRAM
First Baptist, Dallas	1898	Cosmopolitan; tenth largest American city	Bible belt; Evangelistic milieu	Every service	Immersion	Yes, but not major in relation to other church programs
Thomas Road	1956	Bible belt; small city; lower middle class	Fundamentalist	Every service	Immersion	Yes, but not major in relationship to emphasis on other programs
Coral Ridge	Early 1960s	Retirement and winter retreat composed 1/4 of citizens over 60. Medium age 39 years	Secularist with a fairly strong evangelical emphasis	Never	Infant and sprinkling	A major program with more than 300 adults enrolled in outreach

Peninsula Bible	1948	College age (total college enrollment of 34,500 in Palo Alto); 75 percent of congregation under 25	Academic community	Not regular	Not emphasized	Not in major way
Fellowship	1972	Upper middle class	Evangelistic	Not regular	Not emphasized	Only out of house churches
Garden Grove		Stable middle class	Secular/Evangelical	No	Sprinkling/Effusion	No
First Evangelical		Middle	Non-churched community	Not regular	Immersion	Not as major church program
Your Church						

3
Church Growth and Self-Awareness

It is becoming common to find industry and businesses spending sums of money just to help their corporate executives and officers find out about themselves. Since leadership is always the standard and symbol of the organization it directs, this kind of money and time is well spent. The pastor of the church is always the congregational symbol of leadership, love, and counsel.

But most of us struggle with being a symbol, somehow preferring to be a sheep rather than a shepherd. We decry the messianic awe that comes from the children in Vacation Bible School. We are not much at home with new widows, desperate for balance in their grief, and listening to us as though we contain some supernatural offering of stability. Polonius' advice "To thine own self be true" is superfluous. It is not hard being true to ourselves; the trick is to find out who we are and then to apply discipline to our rough, raw, basic ego and shape it so it can become an adequate model or symbol for the church.

It is always honest to point beyond ourselves to Christ as the true Shepherd, the infallible Word of God. But that honesty is usually unavailing. Much of the congregation will still view us with more than humanity at times. They will not reach out to us but up to us. We then must be the shepherd, the symbol to the sheep. How can we struggle to make the model more adequate, for all its sin and humanity and struggle?

Sculpting your own ego is a myopic kind of art. You must be a growing person to pastor a growing church. An ego retreating from discipline, exercise, and growth will soon grow content with its own pettiness. So let's begin by examining your individuality. The following list contains some specific gifts that are yours as a pastor in search of your finest self. This list should be read with a pencil so that you can check or write down the gifts that are yours.

How do you define your temperament?

Sanguine: *The Enjoying Temperament*
Pastors with this temperament are warm, buoyant, and receptive toward their world and enjoy life. They have an ability to live in the present and are accompanied by the it's-great-to-be-alive mystique. They are sometimes subject to flights of unreliability and superficiality and flaring anger. They are weak-willed and find self-discipline hard, in spite of their optimism.

Choleric: *The Active, Practical Temperament*
Pastors with this temperament are strong-willed, self-motivated, and directed. They are practical, keen of mind, bold, and decisive. They are often impatient with the indecisive or the overly sensitive. They tend to be vengeful and are usually haughty and arrogant about their accomplishments.

Melancholy: *The Suffering Temperament*
Pastors with this temperament have a rich and sensitive nature. They are faithful and loyal. They are usually dependable. But they are unhappy and irritable. They have lots of feelings of inner conflict over their own inability to live up to their idealism.

Phlegmatic: *The Calm Temperament*
Pastors in this group always appear cool and undismayed. They face catastrophe without dismay. They are good-natured and great listeners, for they rarely are in a hurry. But they do tend to be slow, lazy, and indigent.

Preaching ability: Excellent; Good; Fair.
Relational gifts: Excellent; Good; Fair.
Do you feel a need for more study and scholarship?

Are you fascinated with:
  Greek exegesis?
  Studying Bible commentaries?
Do you see teaching as a strength?
How about your creativity?
  Do you like art?
  Are you artistic?
  Do you like drama?
  Do you like acting?
  What sort of literature do you like to read?
  Do you read poetry?
  Do you write it?

How about athletic activities?
  Which sports do you enjoy watching?
  In which do you enjoy participating?
How do you view your administrative skill?
Are you good at counseling?
Do you feel that you have sales and motivational ability?
Do you feel your education is adequate to your calling?
Do you need more education?   formal or informal?
What are your hobbies?
Do you make time for them regularly?

Once you arrive at the kind of person you are with a keen awareness of your strengths and weaknesses, then you need to take a look at your community, realizing that all communities will be different. Their individuality must be understood and their needs met if you desire to grow a church in that community. The differences that exist between rural and urban congregations and between the differing kinds of suburbs will demand differing kinds of pastoral leadership. What works in a military community will be ineffective in a university town. What works in a shipyard city will not be effective in a mountain resort, and so forth.

Church growth will be reflected in your understanding of your community. With a pencil and paper, let us repeat the exercise that we did in examining our personality and repeat the same steps in evaluating our community:

Average price of houses in your community:
within a one-mile radius _____
within a three-mile radius _____
within a five-mile radius _____

Nature of the community:
1. White-collar clerical
2. Blue-collar industrial
3. University residential
4. Military or military related
5. Government and civil service installation
6. Resort area
7. Retirement area
8. Junior executive
9. Professional area
   one-mile radius _____
   three-mile radius _____
   five-mile radius _____

The religious character of your field. Estimate what percentage of your area is:
1. Catholic
2. Protestant
3. Jewish
4. Fervent Evangelical
   (Here list charismatic congregations, Baptists, Independent Bible churches, and others noted for their evangelistic outreach.)
   one-mile radius _____
   three-mile radius _____
   five-mile radius _____

The predominant sociological needs of your community:
1. Young working families needing baby-sitting/preschool services.
2. Retirement families trying to adjust to latter-life moves.
3. Underprivileged, welfare, and lower socioeconomic areas.
4. Military communities with counseling needs resulting from family separation and military duties.
5. Resort area where money and appetites may create tremendous needs for help and counseling.
   one-mile radius _____
   three-mile radius _____
   five-mile radius _____

Peter Wagner says that churches grow by homogenous units, and certainly we would have to say that the sociology of church growth cannot be ignored. Therefore, as the next step in the process of church growth, we need to find out just how well we are equipped to handle the task of church growth in the particular field in which we have been called to serve.

Again it is time to put the pencil to our personality and our community. On pages 40–41 appear a chart juxtaposing the pastor's personal abilities and community needs. Please fill in the required blanks as honestly as possible.

Now the issue that must be faced if we use Wagner's term *homogenous* is what I would call the *homogeneity gap*. This is perhaps the most crucial gap for denominational groups as they move from a geographical area of strength to a geographical area of weakness. Usually no attempt is made to honestly assess what the community needs and what the pastor or church can do to meet those needs. Always there will be a gap between the pastors' interests and abilities and the communities' needs and disposition. But once that gap becomes defined in the mind of the pastor, the bridges can be built.

One of the foremost aspects of the gap that I found immediately upon moving to our part of the city had to do with my own income. The church and the Home Mission Board of our Convention were not able to pay me a salary adequate to the salary level of the community where I wanted to start a church. Hence we were not able to live in the community where the church later came to be built. Even six years after we had gone there to build a church, we were not able to afford the kind of home which existed in the immediate area where our church had been constructed.

On the other hand, I felt that my education was adequate to the educational level of those people among whom I wished to build a church.

But at the point of my style of leadership and the type of residents of the West Omaha community, I felt a tremendous tension. My pastoral style had some relational aspects, but my own authoritative pulpit style came through very loud and clear in my views of church administration. I feel that in many ways this is in conflict with the kind of executive and professional congregation into which I was seeking to establish a church. Along the way the tension has surfaced again and again, and I have always felt that I was across the homogeneity gap from the well-educated, executive congregation that I have.

Part of the reason that it is working is that I have learned to make some of the necessary adjustments—and some of them just in the nick of time to ward off church problems in the administration area.

The relational side of my leadership wears well, but its authoritative aspect is too dogmatic and sometimes abusive to make me an effective counselor. So I have simply learned to refer all systematic counseling to someone else. This in a sense contributes to the overall efficiency of my view. Since I realize that a good systematic counselor-pastor tends to be tied up a great deal of his time with a few needy situations, I feel that I can best reach for members on a wider basis if I refer counselees rather than instruct them or counsel them personally.

But the greatest part of the homogeneity gap that I had to cross had to do with discovering my acute minority status as a Southern Baptist. As I said in the introduction, only one-half of 1 percent of the population of Omaha, Nebraska, is Southern Baptist.

I found myself trying to reach people for Christ in a city that was solidly Lutheran and Catholic. So I found out all I could about the doctrines of both churches. I reread everything by Luther I could get my hands on and many books on Catholicism, including the Baltimore Catechism, which I have annotated and keep in my study. The Baltimore Catechism is not a current Catholic favorite, but many of the Catholics I counsel were educated in it and know it.

I found I could build certain bridges in my own thinking.

PASTOR'S PERSONAL ATTRIBUTE	COMMUNITY CHARACTER OR NEED	PASTORAL COMPATIBILITY	PASTORAL DEFICIENCY
Salary of pastor: ___	Average salary of residents around church: ___	Note here if pastor's salary adequate and/or about same: ___	Pastor's salary lower or higher? ___
Pastor's education: List diplomas and degrees: ___	Average level of education of the community resident: ___	Educational level about the same? ___	Pastor significantly over- or undereducated: ___
Pastor's style of leadership:	Predominant employment of the community:	Note where style of leadership does not coincide with the community personnel:	Suggest adjustment:
Relational and democratic	University, white-collar junior executive, professional		
Authoritative	Blue-collar, union, civil service, socially deprived, military		

			Suggest technique for reaching across denominational lines: ___
		Can church grow by ledger additions? ___ Can church grow only by conversion growth? ___	
Casual and unstructured	Artists, actors, resort area, retirement village	Predominant religion of area: ___	
Counseling and relational	Welfare area, predominantly singles community, high divorce area, resort area, underprivileged, or military area, community besieged by problems of rootlessness or family separation	Denominational affiliation of pastor: ___	
		Are they compatible? ___	
	Community attractions and leisure institutions:		
	Pastor's hobbies and interests:		

The literature of the contemplatives had always been a favorite of mine. I no longer felt that I should exclude it from my preaching. I quoted, and still do, from many of my contemplative heroes. I found that I also could incorporate some of the liturgical calendar—notably, the Advent and Holy Week season—into our church. We also had Whitsunday services. I was able to make friends with a born-again priest, and I have borrowed over and over again from his excellence. Our rapport has helped me in presenting Christ to the non-Christian Catholics who exist in my sphere of service to the city.

Further, I decided that since preaching was one of my stronger attributes, it coincided nicely with the emphasis on Christian education for adults. Lutherans and Catholics have very little Bible study emphasis beyond confirmation for adults. So we began with worship; and while it was a different style than they were used to, they could relate far better with worship than adult Sunday School, which was unknown to them. One of the faults of this emphasis is that while our worship has grown fairly fast, our Sunday School emphasis, which includes a healthy discipleship emphasis, is always lagging sadly behind.

To really gain a "picturized" view of your community, take a map and try to see what insight you can gain from the nature of your community. As I began our church in West Omaha, my map of the city became blazoned in my mind. It led me to the firm conviction that it is not possible to build a community Baptist church in Omaha and expect it to grow to any appreciable size. This understanding forced me to consider that the church we were beginning was going to have to make an attempt to reach a considerably larger portion of the city than those who lived within a three-mile radius of the church. As I stated in the introduction to this book, the knowledge that there were twelve times more Jews (and that numerically the Jews were a distinct minority) in our half of the city than there were Southern Baptists naturally led me to form a concept of ministry that was going to have to reach further than our immediate environs to build any kind of Baptist church.

METROPOLITAN OMAHA
APPROXIMATED CHURCH CENSUS
1978

NUMBER OF CHURCHES IN METROPOLITAN OMAHA: 408

Baptist:	68	Membership
Bapt. .... Breakdown:		
SBC 7		3,518
ABC 7		4,682
BGC 6		
GARB 7		
Indep 2		
Other 39		
Lutheran:	56	37,000
Catholic:	51	174,000
Presbyterian:	31	15,567
Methodist:	24	17,744
Christian and Church of Christ:	35	not available

Number and kinds of churches within a 5-mile radius of Westside Baptist Church

Baptist	7 Churches		
Methodist	5 Churches		
Presbyterian	5 Churches		
Lutheran	11 Churches		
Catholic	6 Churches		
Other	10 Churches	Total:	44 Churches

In the yellow pages of our city telephone directory (population 600,000 plus), there were sixty-eight Baptist churches listed. But the combined membership of those churches was only 12,000 people or about 154 members each. Nine of the sixty-eight churches were Southern Baptist with a combined membership of less than 2,000 or around 180 members per church.

Further, my map of the areas revealed that the overwhelmingly nonevangelical census of the city was further complicated by the fact that the city as a whole had very few Southern Baptists being transferred in because of the nature of our middle-class economy, based on sound smaller industry and white-collar executive business of one sort or another. My own maps of the city yielded the following information about our residential constituency.

From this information on both the metropolitan religious census and on our own religious survey conducted several years ago, we were able to put together the following schematics on the religious milieu of our specific community. It will be noted that where the city as a whole is 29 percent Catholic and about 9 percent Lutheran, our specific community survey shows a much heavier concentration of these faiths. In our area of the city 62 percent of the homes had at least one Catholic adult living in them, and an astounding 19 percent had at least one Lutheran adult living there. While these may or may not represent solidly Catholic and Lutheran homes, they are an indicator of the kind of neighborhood in which we are trying to build a church.

This kind of survey information is extremely important to the pastor who desires to grow a church. By learning these kinds of things about your community you become knowledgeable about your field.

In understanding both your field and yourself, you have laid the foundation for church growth.

4
Digging In or "Is There Any Real Hope of Growing an Indigenous Church in a Mobile Society?"

I am haunted by the van lines of our nation. They bring me deacons and steal them away in one year. They take my brightest converts and leave me with empty houses.

The suburbs are good for the children.
A child needs clean air and a yard
And a barbeque pit and a gaslight
We certainly tried very hard
To buy a home next to a negro
Or other race, color or creed.
God knows we adore integration,
But everyone knows children need
The feeling of roots that a rec room
And genuine oak-paneled den
Can offer to split level households
In places called Bonnie Brea Glen,
Where wall-to-wall fires are burning
In family rooms floored in parquet
. . . .
Where civic clubs meet every Friday
And girl scouts watched birds in the park
And even if you went out looking
You couldn't get mugged after dark.
With four walk-in closets to walk in
Three bushes, two shrubs and one tree,
The suburbs are good for the children,
But no place for grown-ups to be. *(Judith Viorst)*

I often add that the suburbs are no place for the indigenous church to be.

Perhaps we need to rethink the word *indigenous*. According to the Britannica Dictionary, its synonyms are *native, innate, inherent*. In a world where population, trends, and traditions are fluid, the search for anything indigenous is frustrating and unrewarding. Recall these indigenous items: the Edsel, the *Saturday Evening Post,* the MacGuire Sisters, the Studebaker, Mickey Mouse, and cyclamates? These things once adhered to the sociological fabric, but they are no longer inherent in our culture.

Churches may be likewise adherent—iron-on patches rather than stitched-in pieces.

With one-fifth of Americans moving every year, it is a challenge to find an "indigenous suburb," let alone an "indigenous suburban church." The suburban church, like suburbia itself, is composed of commercial and industrial transients.

Can any church therefore be said to be native to its suburban setting? Can it be as indigenous as the suburban elementary school, which is also filled with suburbanites? Of course it can. The suburbs of Atlanta and Dallas are full of Baptist churches, as indigenous as the schools and shopping malls.

But the traditional areas of Southern Baptist influence are not my primary interest. My specific issue is: Can we build stable, indigenous suburban churches in areas unfamiliar with Baptist household words (Broadman, Life and Work Curriculum, Lottie Moon)?

Realistically, we are not doing well. Many churches in our pioneer areas are only as inherent as the military or industrial establishment. When the Air Force base or the computer plant closes, the church dwindles and in some cases dies. Where a church grows and atrophies with the waxing and waning of such economic institutions, we must conclude that that church is not indigenous. Only when such churches are composed of members with varied occupational backgrounds will the church be really indigenous.

In most new areas cross-sectional constituency is impossible to arrive at. Nearly every suburban community will have a few families who were saved and baptized somewhere in Dixie. So a mission may begin with a call for transfers of membership. But only a few missions will grow steadily with only such ledger additions. Those churches near an expanding military post or a booming industrial development can grow in this manner. Suburban churches in pioneer areas must meet these challenges to become "dug-in" institutions: *mobile society, cleavages in the city,* and *secular preoccupation.*

1. Mobile Society

This is enemy number 1. In suburban areas one of every four or five houses changes hands every year. With so many people moving out, a growing church must consistently add members faster than it subtracts them.

Our church, for instance, began as a home fellowship of six families. None of these families are still members of the fellowship. Another Nebraska church showed over two hundred additions in one year—but still came up with a net loss of thirteen members.

Mobile membership also produces lonely leadership. Recently our Training Union director and the chairman of our trustees conceived an exciting strategy for advancing the church in six months. Their ideas were great. I felt exhilaration about what God was going to do at Westside in Omaha. Like Moses at the Red Sea, I was itching to divide the difficulties and lead on to victory. Then the Training Union director said, "Pastor, I'm being transferred to Kansas City next month." Not to be outdone, the trustee said, "Don't count on me. If I get my promotion, I'll be in Chicago permanently." So we wait at the starting line until the nominating committee can cover the resignations.

But this frustration is different only in kind from that loneliness which is affecting the layman:

The most virulent poison created by industrial society is excessive loneliness. Our way of life uproots people, carries them upward or downward in the struggle for success. Human bonds are pulverized. Those who cling to family ties are soon left behind in the economic struggle. Those who press forward find themselves cut off from friends and associates. We are the uprooted.[1]

In ministering to the "uprooted" the suburban church must appear to be indigenous. People who spend much of their lives watching the moving men pack their household items need to feel that their church membership is moored. William H. Whyte, Jr., in his book *Organization Man,* tells us why. A nursery in Park Forest, Illinois, advertised that their bushes could be easily transplanted because every year in the nursery the shrubs were transplanted and therefore never developed many roots. This technique made the bushes easy to replant with a minimum of risk to the plant. Mr. Whyte suggests that this is the picture of the *Organization Man* (alias the suburbanite); he develops many short friendships but no long-term ones that would affect his well-being when uprooted.

Even in the church this can be true. The suburbanite is often reluctant to get involved in the fellowship of the church because he hates the amputation from friends when the next promotion comes. He is unintentionally duplicit. He wants his church to be indigenous, but he cannot afford indigenous habitation himself.

2. Cleavages in the City

In a book called *City Politics,* Edward G. Banfield and James Q. Wilson outline urban cleavages:

1. Center city versus the suburbs.
2. Haves versus have-nots.
3. Ethnic tensions, i.e., whites versus negroes.
4. The competition between political parties.[2]

Cleavages in the suburbs are as real, though less traumatic. A list of suburban cleavages might be: (1) Well-paid laborers living beside poorly paid professional and junior executives; (2) School district A versus school district B; may be friendly athletic rivalries or heated issues of educational tax-funding; (3) Apartment dweller versus individual home owner.

Usually these cleavages are not audible but occasionally you hear an exchange such as:

Apartment Tenant: "Come over and swim in my pool, Jim." (Jim is barely a middle-class home owner, whose new but modest home doesn't even have a half bath off the master bedroom.)

Home Owner: "You must let the children come over and play in our sandbox."

Such exchanges are damaging because of an impersonal togetherness. John wouldn't consider asking the carpool members to dinner at his home. After all, his office is two feet longer than theirs, and his salary is better; they are seatbelt buddies, not dinner partners (or fellow church members).

The impersonal nature of suburban life causes many churchmen to withdraw safely to their side of the cleavage and stay there. Witnessing to the iron worker is unthinkable to the college professor (who secretly resents that his house is not quite as nice or his salary as high).

Roger Shinn illustrates this impersonalism: "I remember when the postman delivered a Christmas card signed with a name that no one in the family recognized. The man who sent it guessed that we would not recognize it because under his name he wrote, 'Your Milkman.' " [3]

Several times church members have said, "Pastor, I wish you would go and see Mr. X. He needs to come to Christ. I would ask him myself, but we work together." Or two people from the same office each sit in church, stunned to see each other.

They had no idea that they would be in the same worship service. They work in the same office and thus never talk about those kinds of things.

These cleavages may be more apparent than actual. But such deterrents to close fellowship make it difficult for the church to be stable, inherent to all the variously committed suburbanites.

3. The Secular Preoccupation

Preoccupation with secular pursuits is listed last because it is the most ominous threat to the indigenous suburban church (or any church anywhere). More and more, there is apathy toward the church and fascination with the secular. In 1967 I wrote my assessment in these words:

I Love the Suburbs

I love the suburbs
With curly drives named things like
    Briardale Lane and Foxbury Hunt
The elite cul-de-sacs named things like
    Dublin Circle and Camelot Court.
I love the tracts of Valencia Provincial,
    Rural Swiss, Gabled Icelandic, Cantonese,
Neo-Salsburg houses all in the same block,
    like pavilions at the World's Fair.
I love my neighbor who offers me beer when
    I'm mowing my lawn,
He likes the way I offer him Pepsi when he's
    mowing his.
I love the mustachioed, pipe-smoking history
    teacher with the mini-bike and the maxi-wife.
I love the John Birchers who meet down the block
    with "Your-country-love-it-or-leave-it"
    stickers all over their cars.

I love the sacrificial ways that suburbanites eat
Spaghetti-O's for lunch so they can afford
fondue for dinner.
I love the suburbs because
I love spraying dandelions, playing bridge,
PTA carnivals, anchovies, and pizza,
soap operas, the Wall Street Journal,
Penney's Christmas catalogue, G-movies and
Johnny Carson.
I'm mad about all these things,
so I love the suburbs.

These things all contribute to the secular preoccupation in
the suburbs. Notice there is no mention of the church.

The suburban reaction to the church's outreach is varied. Hostility is infrequent. Apathy is commonplace. The totally secular man may not know how to ask about spiritual things: "The blunt question, 'What the Hell are you doing here?' may be the way in which twentieth-century man asks, 'What must I do to be saved?' " [4]

One of our ladies out on morning visitation was asked this very question by a man who answered the door in his underwear.

I was amazed recently by a woman in the church. She has never taken a teaching position or sung in the choir, although she sings beautifully. She always said she was too busy with sororities, clubs, and her career. But at Christmastime she walked all over her subdivision, asking home owners to use blue lights in their outside Christmas fixtures. She wanted to attract the lighting award committee to her neighborhood.

Her "blue-light drive" was relatively successful—maybe because she demonstrated apostolic zeal. Should I ask her to do the same amount of walking and knocking on doors for a church canvass, she would be "too busy."

Secular pursuits, then, keep many suburbanites from being involved in any attempt at church planting, indigenous or otherwise. Growing a mission church, then, will depend upon athletic stamina. Only those fired by evangelistic zeal can successfully overcome all three difficulties.

Notes

1. Gibson Winter, *Love and Conflict* (New York: Doubleday and Company, Inc., 1958), p. 183.

2. Edward G. Banfield and James Q. Wilson, *City Politics* (Cambridge: Harvard University Press, 1963).

3. Roger Shinn, *Tangled World* (New York: Charles Scribner's Sons, 1965), p. 53.

4. Harvey Cox, *God's Revolution and Man's Responsibility* (Valley Forge: Judson Press, 1965), p. 75.

Planning to Succeed

5
Basic Propositions

(John 21:1–6)

Growing churches requires stamina. But if stamina were the only requirement, then the job could best be done by an ox. So let's review a very few simple principles. Somewhere near the top of the list, write "generosity."

In a survey of congregations in the eastern United States, people were asked to name the most desirable quality of a minister. You think of all the charismatic attributes: zeal, dogma, oratory, personal appearance. But the overwhelming reply was "generosity."

This is synonymous with a giving spirit. Growing churches demand a fervent spirit of giving. Churches grow fastest when the question "What's in this for me?" never occurs to the pastor. You are the sacrifice, the gift, the currency which will be spent.

The spirit of your giving must begin and end in unquestioning obedience. Why let down the nets on the other side of the boat? Because Christ commands it, and he is Lord of the church. Many pastors fish all night and catch nothing. Some fish all their lives and catch nothing. They cannot see that switching from port to starboard can make a difference.

The Bible contains the methodology for catching fish. But the plan is rooted in an understanding that God owns all the fish in every sea.

This sounds elementary! Of course God owns all fish! But most fishermen get possessive when they return with a big catch. They clean and scale; they wrap and hawk the fish in the streets. They pocket all the money. And finally they begin to imagine that *all the fish are theirs!*

Most of us pastors never overcome our possessiveness. We are so used to being in charge that we have a false sense of our own adequacy.

I will never forget the occasion when we christened our first bus, rather like the *Queen Mary* sliding down the ramp into the wonderful world of children. It lurched out of the church parking lot on patched tires and in a cloud of smoke. One month and three repair bills later, I realized that that christening had really been the birth of the blues. I was guilty of doing my own thing at the expense of Christ's:

"Hey, Lord, look! I'm fishing on my side of the boat."

"Yeah, verily, but thou art catching nothing."

"Yeah, but look, Lord, I'm a fisherman—I got this degree. And I photograph so well on the port side."

"But the fish are on the starboard side. Follow me and I will make you a fisher of men."

Without this starboard obedience, you have no power to grow his church.

Once we accept the thesis of God's ownership we need to remember that God has the right to demand anything of us he wishes. Nothing God asks is unreasonable.

Many fishermen gainsay his order to let down the nets on the other side; it seems so futile. They have cast them a thousand times on the portside. They fish and find nothing. Christ shouts over the waves the question:

"Have you taken any meat?"

"No, Lord," we cry. "We've fished the port side for three miles and have caught nothing!"

"Cast your net on the starboard side."

And at his word the nets are logged with the product of our obedience.

In 1970 Oral Roberts published a book called *Seed Faith*, which sold over a million copies. Roberts' thesis was that we plant seed by divine command. It is good seed from which meal or flour could be ground and bread baked. But what would happen if you were to eat up all the seed wheat? We must commit some of it to the ground again if we are not to starve.

Here is the point where Christians are not obedient to God's command. We have his word in Malachi; if we give God every loaf, he will bless us. And consider this promise: "Give, and it shall be given unto you; good measure, pressed down, and shaken together, and running over, shall men give into your bosom. For with the same measure that ye mete withal it shall be measured to you again" (Luke 6:38).

"For if you give, you will get! Your gift will return to you in full and overflowing measure, pressed down, shaken together to make room for more, and running over. Whatever measure you use to give—large or small—will be used to measure what is given back to you" (Luke 6:38, TLB).

If you offer the little sum with obedience, God will return it a hundredfold. He bought you and paid for you and forgave your every sin. He commands, "Give! It will be given back to you!"

Do Christians sow and reap? Do they give? No. God says give, and they will not. God does not in return withhold his blessings. *But why should he have to force-feed you his blessings?* Remember the Russian prisoners who wouldn't eat in the *Gulag Archipelago?* They went on hunger strikes to kill themselves or embarrass their Communist overlords. Solzhenitsyn described forced feeding:

> Artificial feeding has much in common with rape. And that's what it really is: Four big Gulag men hurl themselves on one weak being and deprive it of its one interdiction—they only need to do it once, and what happens to it next is not important. The element of rape inheres in the violation of the victim's will: "It's not going to be the way you want it, but the way I want it; lie down and submit." They pry open the mouth with a flat disc, then broaden the crack between the jaws and insert a tube. "Swallow it." And if you don't swallow it, they shove it farther down anyway and pour liquified food right down

the esophagus. And then they massage the stomach to prevent the prisoner from vomiting. The sensation is one of being morally defiled, of sweetness in the mouth and a jubilant stomach gratified to the point of delight.

Science did not stand still, and other methods were developed for artificial feeding: an enema through the anus, drops through the nose.[1]

So often God has to treat us just this way. We are so stubborn that he has to hold us down, pry our lives open, and force his abundance on us.

God always multiplies, but he multiplies only what we give him. If we give nothing, he multiplies it and gives it back. But anything times zero is zero. Give him nothing, and multiplied it still yields nothing.

So when God demands that we fish from the starboard side, we must obey. Empty nets are the result of self-will. I pray that you will not be an illustration of Gail Brook Burket's poem, *Paradox:*

> Men call me Master but will not obey;
> Good Shepherd yet delight to go astray;
> The Sun of Righteousness but choose the night;
> The Truth yet put my precepts from their sight;
> The Way but follow other paths through life;
> The Prince of Peace yet foment war and strife;
> A Sure Foundation, while they build on sand;
> The King of Kings and spurn my great command.
> Men call me Lord and Savior even now,
> Who press the thorns of hatred on my brow.[2]

Let's talk about the rhythm of *obedience* and *blessing.* "Beloved, I wish above all things that thou mayest prosper and be in health, even as thy soul prospereth. [That's God's wish for your life.] I have no greater joy than to hear that my children walk in truth" (3 John 2:4).

Remember the seed principle; the farmer takes good wheat

and commits it to the ground. He doesn't stand there and marvel that it grows—he expects it to grow.

In my early years of fishing, the fish were sparser. Slowly, ever so slowly, I began to learn the cycles of obedience and blessing. When I obeyed the Father, I could expect the fishing to improve. It was amazing how my expectations grew.

For the sake of illustration let us repeat an old story about B. H. Carroll. He was preaching in a seminary chapel on soul-winning and having a compassionate heart. His delivery was stirring. After the sermon, a young seminarian came up and confessed that while he desperately wanted to see people saved, it just never happened in his church. Carroll said, "Well, son, in your little rural church with so few people, you don't expect people to be saved every time you preach, do you?"

"No," said the seminarian. "I don't."

"That," said the old saint, "is exactly why they are not saved every time you preach."

I anticipate Sunday morning in our church. The mood is electric. The Holy Spirit is there. Why shouldn't I expect something in the nets? When the blessings are on, I fish myself weak; I can't stop. I'm a fishaholic! Life in Christ really becomes beautiful when you are in a life-cycle of obedience.

Now read this passage carefully: "So I have asked these other brothers to arrive ahead of me to see that the gift you promised is on hand and waiting. I want it to be a real gift and not look as if it were being given under pressure. But remember this— if you give little, you will get little. A farmer who plants just a few seeds will get only a small crop, but if he plants much, he will reap much. Every one must make up his own mind as to how much he should give. Don't force anyone to give more than he really wants to, for cheerful givers are the ones God prizes. God is able to make it up to you by giving you everything you need and more, so that there will not only be enough for your own needs, but plenty left over to give joyfully to others. It is as the Scriptures say, 'The godly man gives generously to

the poor. His good deeds will be an honor to him forever.'
For God, who gives seed to the farmer to plant, and later on,
good crops to harvest and eat, will give you more and more
seed to plant and will make it grow so that you can give away
more and more fruit from your harvest. Yes, God will give you
much so that you can give away much" (2 Cor. 9:5–11, TLB).

God gives the increase for us to pass on.

But we're greedy, aren't we? Affluence is our way of life, and
we think the increase is rightly ours. The resulting tragedy is
a false view that we are self-sufficient. Occasionally someone
reminds us that God is still the owner of all. We will be account-
able for any discrepancy in the gifts received and forwarded.

There is to be no end or limit to our giving. Howard Hendricks
records this experience.

> A number of us who were speaking there went across the
> street at noon to get a bite to eat at the hamburger stand.
> The place was crowded and people were standing in line. An
> elderly lady was in front of me. I guessed she was about 65—
> she was 83, I learned later. She wore a convention badge, so
> I knew she was a conferee. There was a table for four open,
> so two friends and I invited her to join us.
>
> I asked her the obvious question, "Do you teach a Sunday
> School class?"
>
> "Oh, I certainly do," she said.
>
> I visualized a class of senior citizens and asked, "What age
> group do you teach?"
>
> "I teach a class of junior high boys."
>
> "Junior high boys! How many boys do you have?"
>
> "Thirteen," she said sweetly.
>
> "Tremendous! I suppose you come from a large church."
>
> "No, sir, it's very small," she said, "we have about 55 in
> Sunday School."
>
> Hardly daring to go on, I said, "What brings you to this
> Sunday School Convention?"
>
> "I'm on a pension—my husband died a number of years
> ago," she replied, "and frankly, this is the first time a conven-

tion has come close enough to my home so I could afford to attend. I bought a Greyhound ticket and rode all last night to get here this morning and attend two workshops. I want to learn something that will make me a better teacher." [3]

Obedience and blessing. Never quit giving until we stand in his presence. And as you give, expect God to give!

Notes

1. Aleksandr I. Solzhenitsyn, *The Gulag Archipelago* (New York: Harper & Row, 1973), p. 470.

2. Gail Brook Burket, *Paradox* (Evanston, Illinois).

3. Howard G. Hendricks, *Say It with Love* (Wheaton: Victor Books, 1972), pp. 46–47.

6
The Importance of Personal Goals

I recently heard a motivational speaker say that 65 percent of all adults have no formula for approaching life. They drift along on business as usual. All their goals are short-term. Thursday night they are dining with the Joneses. Saturday night they will play bridge with the Smiths; and Sunday, of course, they'll spend the day at the lake. But don't ask them about next month or next year. Above all, don't ask them where they plan to be in a decade. They haven't planned for that.

The speaker went on to say that perhaps 5 percent of adults ever write their goals on paper. Ninety-five percent have "goal myopia." But the Bible says: "Where there is no vision the people perish" (Prov. 29:18). Because of our preoccupation with the contemporary scene, most of us collide with the future. Why not have a planned encounter?

Doing nothing and dreaming nothing are companion attitudes. Goals and dreams can be agonizing. It is safer not to dream. If you never aim at anything, you cannot miss your mark or know the embarrassment of missing.

Here I must present a great biblical word: *sin!* In the Old Testament the word is *katah;* in the New Testament the word is *hamartia.* Both words mean *to miss the mark.* Romans 3:23 says it best: "For all have sinned and come short of the glory of God." All have "missed the mark." This should cut to the heart. Sin in Scripture is to miss the mark. But *the epitome of sin must be to aim at nothing.*

Now most of us, when we were young, had goals. We wanted:

1. A driver's license
2. A car
3. A high school diploma
4. A college degree
5. A job that paid well.

For probably 80 percent of adults a well-paying job was the final goal. They got the job, started a family, and just never set any more goals.

Paul believed in a good aim. He said, "Forgetting those things which are behind, and reaching forth unto those things which are before, I press toward the mark for the prize of the high calling of God in Christ Jesus" (Phil. 3:13–14). What is your mark? What prize? Clear them with God, and then write the outline for yourself.

Your ultimate goal, of course, should be to be like Christ. But you need to record those things, or that one thing, that you know is the achievement through which Christ will be best reflected in your life. Write it down on paper! Read it twice a day until you have memorized it.

This is a visionary step that requires maturity and judgment. Some ladies will remember when their goal was to be a ballerina. They now stumble to the breakfast table, tripping over their flip-flops, and marvel at that early goal. But our problems as youth lay in the diversity and number of our goals. The growing girl did not want to be *just* a ballerina; she wanted to be a movie star, a novelist, and a fashion model all at the same time.

Men progressed similarly from engineer to fireman, or from policeman to fighting leatherneck. When they made their vocational choices, they may have abandoned the best choice. I've known people in their middle thirties and forties who were not happy. They were still looking for their real vocation in life.

You are a minister of Jesus Christ. Let us assume that your vocation is right. Then your goal is a spiritual one. Before your life is over, you may want to become a dynamic witness. Whatever your goal is, fill in the blank. If you have no idea of where your life is headed, you need to ask yourself this question and begin praying. Pray until you have a vision of what you want to become.

One church member called me some time ago and said, "I have this terrific idea!"

"What is it?" I asked.

"Oh, no! Heh, heh, heh . . . If I told you my terrific idea, you'd get a patent on it and you'd tell everybody it was your idea; and you'd get rich and I wouldn't."

"Look," I said. "I'm a preacher . . . you can trust me."

"Yeah . . . heh . . . heh. I'm writing this great idea in three separate registered letters, and I'm going to mail you one. Don't open it; just leave it sealed in your file."

"OK," I said. "You can trust me."

Now I have that confounded letter in my file. A brainstorm, drawn in detail. Every time I walk by that filing cabinet, I see that letter. It is driving me mad not to know what is in it, but I promised. If my friend dies—mind you, I don't wish him any ill luck—I'll have that letter open before his obituary is in the paper.

He had a great idea and he wrote it down. And he's working on it. It may take him two years to get it operational, and it may take him five. But his whole life is pointed.

Campus Crusade is right. God does love you and has a wonderful plan for your life. He has a destiny for you. He wants to work his creation in you over thirty or forty years; and if you follow through in working his plan, then you will achieve the design of God. Maybe you should write that goal down right now! If you don't know what your goal is, spend time in prayer until it becomes a specific objective in your mind.

Now think for a moment what specific steps you need to take to accomplish your lifetime objective. The steps should also be written. When I took my first pastorate, my goal was to be successful by the time I was thirty years old. I had set a kind of goal for myself, but I hadn't given it very many definitions. Success? What was it? Well, I always wanted to write. So I thought step 1 would be to write a book. I always wanted to give a lecture on Gothic architecture in Luxembourg, so step 2 would be travel. And I always wanted to pastor in the city.

At twenty-eight I began to panic. No publisher had accepted my writing. I had seldom traveled out of Cass County, Nebraska. My ministry required fifteen hours a day, but just wouldn't go anywhere. I was living in a cycle of rejection. I would write a manuscript and send it off. It would come back. I would cry. Barbara, my devoted wife and first fan, would cry and say, "They'll be sorry some day!" We would edit the manuscript and send it off again.

We had to go to Europe if I were to write my lecture on Gothic architecture in Luxembourg. So we ate beans and saved money. After one year I was twenty-nine and on my way to Europe. We took three hundred slides of Gothic buildings in Luxembourg and onion domes in Austria. We visited every important gallery in western Europe and arrived home two months before my thirtieth birthday. Then my first book was accepted by a publisher, and we moved to the city.

But the reality was not what I had imagined. Fifteen or twenty people attended my city church on a big Sunday. Release of my book was still a year away. Nobody wanted to hear my lecture on Gothic architecture in Luxembourg. I was morose and moody for days at a time.

Gradually, I faced the reality. I had a new vision. Perhaps by the time I was forty . . . I was off and running on another ten-year stretch. In my mind I pictured success at forty. Gothic architecture in Luxembourg wouldn't contribute, so I decided to major on evangelism and writing. A good evangelist has to make a lot of calls. A good writer has to be a good reader. I began setting goals for how many calls I was going to make and how many books I was going to read. I set a minimum of twenty-five calls and two books a week. I maintained those goals over eight years and have now substantially increased them.

I learned new facets of success. To have the ministry I want at forty, I have to train many people to do exactly what I do. I believe God put that dream in my heart. I believe that he will use my life to realize this vision.

I have a goal: fifty people on evangelism teams in the next two years. I have a goal: twenty-five deacons making ministry calls to the friends and members of this church. The highlights of my week are ministry meetings where the men and women of this church—deacons and lay witness ministers—accept the challenge to use their lives in this manner.

I believe that God is going to give us the city. We have the talent and dedication, and we are planning our attack now. This is the planning stage of your dream. How are you going to accomplish it? First have the vision and then map the strategy of your conquest.

But a final consideration is the issue of economics. How much will the goal require? What will it cost in time and energy? Luke 14:28–32 says: "For which of you, intending to build a tower, sitteth not down first, and counteth the cost, whether he has sufficient to finish it? Lest haply, after he hath laid the foundation, and is not able to finish it, all that behold it begin to mock him, Saying, This man began to build, and was not able to finish. Or what king, going to make war against another king, sitteth not down first, and consulteth whether he is able with ten thousand to meet him that cometh against him with twenty thousand? Or else, while the other is yet a great way off, he sendeth an ambassage and desireth conditions of peace."

Before you stand to conquer, you must sit down to count the cost. Isolate your vision. Program the possibilities and ask yourself about the cost. Goals take time: hours, weeks, years, decades. They take energy. By the time you have finished you may be old and spent. The plan may take money: literally hundreds of thousands of dollars over your lifetime. How much can you pay? How much will you pay?

Every goal has its critics. How do you handle criticism? How much are you willing to take? I read of a man who wanted more than anything else to become the vice-president of a large company. There was criticism all along the way. But he stuck out his chin and took it all. Finally, he was promoted to that glorious office. Naturally, he was proud and even boasted to his wife, who finally retorted: "Vice-presidents are a dime a dozen. Why, in the supermarket they even have a vice-president in charge of prunes."

Furious, the man phoned the supermarket and asked to speak to the vice-president in charge of prunes. "Which kind?" was the reply. "Packaged or bulk?"

Now it costs nothing to have a vision, but it costs a great deal sometimes to make a vision reality. What *are* visions worth? As a child, my wife cut out a picture of a wedding cake. This was the cake she wanted at her wedding. She kept that picture until it was a challenge to make out what it was. She prayed that someday she would have that cake. She also prayed that someday she would get a man. One day the Lord answered both prayers. She didn't seem to care much about the wedding. Even the groom didn't matter much. But the cake did!

We took the picture to the bakery. The baker said doubtfully, "Well, I don't know that I've ever seen a cake like this!" Barbara nearly broke into tears. Finally he said, "Look, lady, I'll try!" She stuck with her goal, no matter what the cost.

Christ came to redeem the world. He knew from the first what it was going to cost, but he was determined to do all of the Father's will. The Scriptures say, "I set my face like a flint" (Isa. 50:7). He would not be swerved. Because he clung to that vision, we have eternal life. Listen to Isaiah:

"The Lord God hath opened mine ear, and I was not rebellious, neither turned away back. I gave my back to the smiters, and my cheeks to them that plucked off the hair; I hid not my face from shame and spitting. For the Lord God will help me;

therefore shall I not be confounded, therefore have I set my face like a flint, and I know that I shall not be ashamed. He is near that justifieth me; who will contend with me? let us stand together: who is mine adversary? . . . Behold the Lord God will help me; who is he that shall condemn me? . . . Behold, all ye that kindle a fire, that compass yourselves about with sparks: walk in the light of the fire, and the sparks that you have kindled" (Isa. 50:5–11).

Our Savior was willing to pay that price. Think about other men who paid for their vision. Martin Luther King said on August 28, 1963, at a Washington rally:

> I say unto you, my friends, that in spite of difficulties and frustrations of the moment, I still have a dream. It is a dream deeply rooted in the American dream
>
> I have a dream that one day on the red hills of Georgia the sons of former slaves and the sons of former slaveowners will be able to sit down together at the table of brotherhood.
>
> I have a dream that one day even the state of Mississippi, a desert state sweltering with the heat of injustice and oppression, will be transformed into an oasis of freedom and justice.
>
> I have a dream that my four little children will one day live in a nation where they will not be judged by the color of their skin, but by the content of their character.[1]

I have a dream for Omaha, Nebraska. Men and women who love the Lord—Baptist men and women—are going to stand up for what they believe. They will put pettiness and self-seeking aside and go out with God to touch people in need of the saving power of Jesus Christ.

The effort will cost. It will cost at least 10 percent of their income and 100 percent of their commitment to Jesus. It may be staggering in terms of money and effort. But with God, nothing is impossible.

God gives us possible dreams! He wants a great evangelical witness in your city too. The blueprints he has given you existed in his mind in eternity past. Now they are in yours. Tomorrow they will be a reality based on your faithfulness.

Note

1. Harvey Cox, *God's Revolution and Man's Responsibility* (Valley Forge: Judson Press, 1965), p. 59.

7
The Stamina for Dreaming

Joel 2:28; Isa. 40:31

The current generation is confused. We dream, but have trouble deciding which dream to pursue, and even more trouble keeping our dreams from running together like a Salvador Dali "Clockscape!"

The doctrine of election says that a great God is in control of our lives. This great God leaves nothing to happenstance. How did you come to know Christ in the first place? It happened as a result of two events, both God-programmed acts: (1) Jesus' death and (2) your birth. "For from the very beginning God decided that those who came to him—and all along he knew who would—should become like his Son, so that his Son would be the First, with many brothers" (Rom. 8:29, TLB).

God set out years ahead of time not only to save you, but to make you like Jesus. "And having chosen us, he called us to come to Him; and when we came, he declared us 'not guilty,' filled us with Christ's goodness, gave us right standing with himself, and promised us his glory" (Rom. 8:30, TLB). God is going to make a success of you. He already knows what you will look like when your success is ultimate. He sees you saved, sanctified, and glorified. "What can we ever say to such wonderful things as these? If God is on our side, who can ever be against us? Since he did not spare even his own Son for us but gave him up for us all, won't he also surely give us everything else? Who dares accuse us whom God has chosen for his own? Will God? No! He is the one who has forgiven us and given us right standing with himself" (Rom. 8:31–33, TLB).

Seven major passages in the New Testament talk about the completeness of redemption.

God is a planner, the architect of history. Now every Christian is not merely to live a life, but to build a life. You must think architecturally—what can you build with breath and seventy-odd years of experience? Where are your blueprints? How long will the project take to finish? Builders see life in terms of direction and completion.

For instance, the Cologne Cathedral required four hundred years to build. Many generations worked on it. Each understood that they had inherited a dream and that they would pass only a dream to the next generation. The completed cathedral was for a still-more-distant generation. But if you had asked any stonecutter what he was doing, he would not have said, "I am chipping rock." He would have said, "I am building a cathedral."

Once I stood in St. Peter's Square. I looked up at the dome and pondered its history. Michelangelo designed an immense self-supporting dome in the shape of the Pope's triple crown. It was a dream. He knew he would never see it completed. He gave the blueprints to Bernini, who continued the work.

John A. Roebling dreamed of a great bridge to stretch from Brooklyn to the city of New York. In 1867 that was a terrific dream—a 1595½-foot suspension bridge had never been built. When he died his son, Washington Roebling, took his blueprints and began work. In 1869, while sinking the pneumatic piling for the New York pier, he was nearly asphyxiated. He suffered the rest of his life from caisson disease. This paralyzing disease affected his concentration and restricted his activities to short periods. He could scarcely talk and communicated with his wife through symbols and signs. She continued the mathematical computations on the bridge, clarified his calculations, and gave all his orders to the workmen. Roebling watched from his apartment in his pajamas. The work on his dream went on during fourteen years of his convalescence. Some years ago, I drove across the great bridge into Manhattan—what a tribute to a man who wouldn't quit! A man with a blueprint to follow and finish.

Most people never build because they have no blueprints. Would Michelangelo have succeeded without them? Or Roebling? Of course not! You must have a blueprint to build a cathedral, a bridge, or a life. Make a blueprint of how to use your life and structure your dreams, and then follow that plan.

Once you find your dream and your plan, you must program yourself into an "accomplishment system." This programming is something many people never do well. Recently I attended a Christian writer's conference with Sherwood Wirt, the editor of *Decision* magazine. He was addressing a group of would-be writers. Several times during the speech he said, "Never forget this!" Then he slammed the table with his fist and said, "You are a professional . . . you're a writer. You're influencing a great many people through the printed page." Now few, if any, in that room had really done any writing. What was he trying to prove? To be a writer, you have to program yourself to write.

Later, alone with Dr. Wirt, I asked, "Dr. Wirt, how old were you when you wrote your first major book?"

"Forty-eight," he answered, "but I was a serious writer long before that."

You see, he had programmed himself to write something every day. Then I remembered reading that Arthur Haley makes himself write five hundred words every day. If he gets to the end of a day and has not written five hundred words, he stops right there and does it. *To be a writer you have to program yourself to write.*

Years ago I set these goals: Read eight books a month. Make twenty-five visits a week. Write at least one manuscript a year. Now in the last eight years I have read over one thousand books. One year alone, I made over 1,900 house calls, and I commuted between Omaha and Kansas City for five months. Since 1967 I have published one book a year. How do I get this done? I have programmed myself to do it.

Personal programming is interesting. You must program in

all the positive *and* negative aspects of both your short and long-range goals. But whatever you do, do not lose sight of your goal. Build some direct and restrictive system to make you pressure yourself to achieve that goal.

When all is said and done, there is one final thing that you must do: Take a risk. If Evel Knievel had not "popped" his first "wheelie," he certainly would not have jumped all those autos.

See risk as illustrated in Jesus' parable of the talents:

"He gave $5,000 to one, $2,000 to another, and $1,000 to the last—dividing it in proportion to their abilities—and then left on his trip. The man who received the $5,000 began immediately to buy and sell with it and soon earned another $5,000 . . . But the man who received the $1,000 dug a hole in the ground and hid the money for safekeeping. After a long time their master returned from his trip and called them to him to account for his money. The man to whom he had entrusted the $5,000 brought him $10,000. His master praised him for good work. 'You have been faithful in handling this small amount,' he told him, 'so now I will give you many more responsibilities. Begin the joyous tasks I have assigned to you.'. . . . Then the man with the $1,000 came and said, 'Sir, I knew you were a hard man, and I was afraid you would rob me of what I earned, so I hid your money in the earth and here it is!' But his master replied, 'Wicked man! Lazy slave! Since you knew I would demand your profit, you should at least have put my money into the bank so I could have some interest. Take the money from this man and give it to the man with the $10,000. For the man who uses well what he is given shall be given more, and he shall have abundance. But from the man who is unfaithful, even what little responsibility he has shall be taken from him. And throw the useless servant out into outer darkness: there shall be weeping and gnashing of teeth' " (Matt. 25:15–30, TLB).

Think of the adventures inherent in *risk*. Win Arn took some young people to a circus to film a promotional picture. After the performance, he and some of the church youth were standing beneath the trapeze apparatus. One of the young people said, "Brother Arn, could you do that?"

"Sure," he said, "anybody could."

They taunted him until he finally stripped off shoes and jacket and started up the ladder. He said that as he climbed past the safety net it looked broad and wide. But forty-five feet up the ladder the net looked tiny. He thought he could fall and miss it altogether. When he reached the platform and took the swing in his hand, he said he was aware of the little pedestal swaying gently, making him feel seasick and insecure. But he could hear the young people applauding, and it just didn't seem the time to quit.

So he grabbed the swing in both hands and cut an arc into the middle of the silent big top. A professional aerialist started the swing from the other side and Arn suddenly realized something. He could not grasp swing "B" without releasing swing "A." Before he lost both propriety and nerve, he let go of swing "A." He reached out and felt nothing. There was nothing there— just air—for what seemed an eternity. Then in an unforgettable moment, the cold steel bar of the swing tapped his palms. He quickly closed his hands around it and swung to the other side. He said that in that moment he learned everything about the nature of risk.

Risk is a principle of the kingdom of God. Jesus said, "Whosoever will save his life must lose it. He who gives it away will keep it unto life eternal" (Matt. 10:39, author's paraphrase).

As we close this section remember these basic things. First, *God created you uniquely and he created you to win!* Second, *God is not haphazard in running our lives.* Third, *if God is in our hearts, we cannot fail, since his power propels us to victory.*

Here, then, is your application for success. Fill it out. This is only the beginning—an indication that you are aware of your direction. To win at life, trust all you are and have to Jesus Christ. Who knows? Perhaps when you grow, your church will too.

AIM AFFIRMATION:
Desiring to make my life useful to Christ, I establish this goal as my primary life goal. This is the one thing I would supremely like to attain:
_____

AIM ACTUALIZING:
To actualize the attainment of my life aim, I conceive it necessary to take these steps in the order of their prior importance to my final aim:
Step 1: _____
Step 2: _____
Step 3: _____
Step 4: _____
Step 5: _____

AIM ALIGNMENT:
Date, I plan to begin with Step 1 _____
Date, I plan to finish Step 1 _____
Date, I plan to finish Step 2 _____
Date, I plan to finish Step 3 _____
Date, I plan to finish Step 4 _____
Date, I plan to finish Step 5 _____

AIM ACTUALIZING AND AGE OF ATTAINMENT:
I will be _____ years old when I attain Step 1.
I will be _____ years old when I attain Step 2.
I will be _____ years old when I attain Step 3.
I will be _____ years old when I attain Step 4.
I will be _____ years old when I attain Step 5.
By the time I attain Step 5 I will have used up _____ percent of my effective adult life. (Consider ages between twenty and sixty-five to be your effective adult years.)

The Sciences of Church Growth

8
The Theology of Church Growth

Integrate the fingers of your right and left hands inward toward the palms, and recite this ancient parable of church growth: "Here's the church, Here's the steeple; Open the door and see . . . the same old lackluster crowd." On the back pew are the Pinkies, a short, practically useless couple who always station themselves near the rear of the church for a fast exit. On the next row are the Ringmans, an affluent gold-banded couple who must display their material trappings. Next are the Tallmans, impressive and self-important. And at the very front are Brother and Sister Pointer, who furnished the steeple where, of course, we "open the door and see all the people."

Only there aren't very many people. Just the Pinkies, Ringmans, Tallmans, and Pointers. But with just four key families, the lights burn every night at the church. There are forty-two organizations and committees. While all the families have noticed that their church isn't growing (hasn't for years), none of them suspect that there is a relationship between church growth and theology.

When I visited Westminster Abbey several years ago, there was a flower show in the cathedral. At that time the Anglican communion was nearly a nonchurch. Only a tenth of the membership attended regularly. Now it is ludicrous to suggest that Westminster had church growth as even a remote goal. How do you enroll the Archbishop of Canterbury in a Lay Institute of Evangelism? But I have always resented the little old lady who asked our guide, "Has anybody been saved around here lately?" Her question was valid. To be sure, it seems simplistic to look at the graves of England's greatest monarchs and ask such an evangelistic question. The incident points up that for even the Archbishop there is a relationship between church growth and theology.

Before I go further, let me voice one conclusion reached in fifteen years of trying to grow churches: *The only valid principle of church growth is evangelism.* Therefore, a theology for church growth must support evangelism in various forms. Let us examine two opposite approaches, those of the Bishop of Woolwich and Jerry Falwell.

John A. T. Robinson, Bishop of Woolwich, has "demythologized" God. He escaped from a three-story universe into hiding in the warm existentialism of Paul Tillich's *Ground of Being.* He has denuded structures of religious practice and opted for Bonhoeffer's religionless Christianity. Robinson admits that Southern Baptists and Roman Catholics are more authoritative on religion than he is.[1] It has been years since he asked, "Are you saved, brother?"

On the other side of the Atlantic, Jerry Falwell has continued his revivalism by building his college and bus ministry. He not only believes in the three-story universe (the one Robinson rejects), but he runs the elevator that makes regular stops on all three floors. Falwell believes in the virgin birth of Christ, verbal-plenary inspiration of the Scriptures, the premillennial return of Christ, and other basics.

Now the question: Is there an observable relationship between these men and the growth of their churches? Let's take the bishop first. There is nothing evangelical in his approach. He has collected adherents interested in the intrigue of his subject. They are like a group of boys I once saw throwing firecrackers: The boy who could hold the lighted firecracker longest before he threw it was the winner. The danger is obvious, but it does draw a crowd.

But is it Falwell's theology that is drawing the crowd? Are

people so hungry for a three-story world that they will fight the Lynchburg traffic? Or is his attractiveness a subtle blend of the three-story universe and the newest Madison Avenue technique? For all his techniques, my sympathies and my theology lie nearer Falwell than Robinson. Falwell's is in essence a theology of church growth.

I am reluctant to abandon the metaphors of Scripture. I confess I generally speak of heaven as up, hell as down, and Chicago as east of Omaha. I do not worry about transgressing geophysics by doing this any more than I worry about transgressing cardiology when I speak to a child of "letting Jesus come into his heart." The Bishop of Woolwich may not understand; apparently the only way Christ could get into his heart is through the aorta. I would like to suggest a proper theology for church growth. A church will grow if its theology is orthodox, urgent, and simple.

1. An Orthodox Theology

For want of a better definition I see orthodoxy as adherence to those doctrines formerly called "fundamentals": (1) verbal-plenary inspiration, (2) the virgin birth of Christ, (3) the sinless life of Christ, (4) the resurrection and ascension, (5) the premillennial return of Christ, (6) heaven and hell, and (7) blood atonement. Do you react to this statement of fundamentals? I believe any serious study would reveal *most* of these precepts as underlying the theology of growing churches.

Dean Kelley's conclusions support this view. Remember that Kelley himself is an official of the National Council of Churches and a Methodist minister. Still he concludes:

> For precisely the sectarian and theologically conservative religious groups have made amazing gains in recent years. Amid the current neglect and hostility toward organized religion in general, the conservative churches, holding to seemingly outmoded theology and making strict demands on their members, have equalled or surpassed in growth the yearly percentage increases in the nation's population.[2]

John Bisagno observes that all of the largest churches in America are "conservative and fundamental."[3] Thomas Howard described the nausea we feel when we examine the jargon that typifies the conservative and fundamental church:

> I was especially careful about terminology . . . the ultimate test of all phraseology was whether or not it included this one: "Accept the Lord Jesus Christ as your personal Savior" . . . I also like the sound of "Christ in you," and "the blood of Jesus Christ," and "millions are perishing," and "what doth it profit a man." I felt these things ought to form the currency of a man's conversation. I listened to ministers to see if they said the correct things. Once a man I knew used the phrase, "the Christ event." I thought, "oh, pshaw. What is this? Clearly he is not born again or he would not be talking that way."[4]

Before we become too critical, let us take a look at the current theological milieu.

Schleiermacher's departure from orthodoxy at the beginning of the nineteenth century spawned many forms of liberalism. From his anthropocentric theology came both social and existential theology. His disciples continued their humanistic and rationalistic writing until the Bible had lost its authority. Other theologians who made their contributions to liberalism were Ritschl, F. C. Baur, Rauschenbusch, Bushnell, etc. Belief in progress and the overcoming humanity of man grew out of optimistic liberalism. But by the middle of World War I, optimistic liberalism was disenchanted.

In those years Karl Barth was pastor at Safenwil. Observing his congregation's despair, he searched for a more meaningful dogma to preach. From this agony of soul he wrote *Romerbrief*, published in 1919 in an edition of one thousand copies. Even this limited edition fell like a "bomb on the playground of European theologians," as Karl Adams said. *Romerbrief* was a summons back to orthodoxy. It built upon Hegel's use of dialectic and Kierkegaard's existentialism. Barth placed dialectical categories in close juxtaposition and talked in the same breath of "eminence and transcendence, or revelation and hiddenness."

None can gainsay Karl Barth his tremendous impact for good. He established a friendly climate for fundamentalists by popularizing their terms Word of God, virgin birth, resurrection, etc. But his orthodoxy was not the same that had existed pre-Schleiermacher. It was a new orthodoxy. Before long American fundamentalists were wary of his dialectic. Why couldn't Barth say virgin birth and leave it at that? Why did he have to talk of "virgin birth sign" or "resurrection sign"? He said he was a Trinitarian, but he was big on God and weak on the Incarnation. He discounted hell, and it showed through his dialectical categorizing.[5] The Bible becomes the Word of God when it speaks to us, he taught. Where it does not speak to us, it may be potentially the Word of God; but it is not presently the Word.

Many commendable things can be said of Barthianism. It is a refreshing turn from the liberalism which preceded it. But it is inadequate as a basis for growing churches. While I have limited experience, I have never known a "Neo-orthodox soul-winner." No, the functional distance between Barth and Jack Hyles is directly proportional to the geographical distance between Basel, Switzerland, and Hammond, Indiana.

What then are we to say? Should we, like Barth, attempt to psych ourselves out? No, but I believe honest appraisal of our doctrinal views might move us a long way in the direction of orthodoxy.

Neo-orthodoxy is a wedding of rationale and faith. We subject any *rera novarum* to the test of reason. Are we right to do this? All Southern Baptists would believe in the literal resurrection of Christ; they might not be as sure about the floating axehead in 2 Kings. But the floating axehead and the resurrection are both issues of faith. The faith to believe in either event differs only in degree—both events must be accepted beyond reason.

The cardinal doctrine is biblical authority. If the Bible is inerrant, reason is no judge in deciding which miracles are credible. To the pure scientist, they are all incredible. To me classic agnosticism and radical orthodoxy are the consistent ways. The classic agnostic would agree that the resurrection and the floating axehead must be examined on the same nonempirical basis. While either is as credible as the other, to him neither is credible. The orthodox theologian would also put the events on the same plane of credibility, would see each as believable, and both as highly likely.

Is this an absurd hypothesis? Floating axeheads and church growth are related. Can one reject the prophet's axe and win souls? Of course. But in practice as in principle, a correlation exists between those who hold orthodox doctrine and those who "win souls" and consequently experience church growth.

Francis Schaeffer, commenting upon what Malcolm Muggeridge called the "great liberal death wish," said:

> He [Muggeridge] simply admitted that he had realized that goal toward which he had been optimistically moving was not going to be realized. The liberalism in which he had his hopes had cut away all the groundwork and left no categories with which to judge.[6]

The great liberal death wish is still rooted in Schleiermacher. It still has man in the center, a magistrate who rules Scripture, giving only select passages permission to speak with authority. The wish is being granted. A computerized projection shows Presbyterians baptizing their last infant in May of 1992 if their decline continues.

The "Great Conservative Life Wish" lies in orthodoxy, that never-never land to which Barth paved the way. He was buried on Nebo, just outside orthodoxy's border. Those who were not afraid of reason and liberalism crossed the boundary and are building the Kingdom on the firm foundation of acceptance.

2. An Urgent Theology

Urgency in any medium provokes action. An insurance man says, "Mr. Smith, you should buy this policy, for someday your house may be on fire." That statement would, however, get less immediate response than should a neighbor appear at Mr. Smith's door and say, "Great Scott, Smitty, *your house is on fire!*"

Growing churches practice an evangelism of urgency. It is easy to forget that the New Testament theology was urgent. The plight of man is couched in desperate terms. "Are you *saved*, Brother?" "Millions are *perishing!*" "This man is *lost!*" In days gone by evangelical hymns focused on our desperation:

> Rescue the perishing, Care for the dying,
> Snatch them in pity from sin and the grave;
> Weep o'er the erring one, Lift up the fallen,
> Tell them of Jesus the mighty to save.

> My soul in sad exile was out on life's sea,
> So burdened with sin, and distressed.

> Out of my bondage, sorrow, and night,
> Jesus, I come.

Whence came this urgency, this desperation? It came from the theology of the New Testament. Jesus used desperate terms to refer to himself—*Savior* or *Deliverer*. He came to deliver a world already condemned (John 3:18). Jesus preached a fiery apocalypticism. Twenty-four times in the Gospels he spoke on fire and brimstone. He said: "The Son of man shall send forth his angels, and they shall gather out of his kingdom all things that offend, . . . and shall cast them into a furnace of fire: there shall be wailing and gnashing of teeth" (Matt. 13:41–42). "Then shall he say also unto them on the left hand, Depart from me, ye cursed, into everlasting fire, prepared for the devil and his angels" (Matt. 25:41).

"I am come to send fire on the earth" (Luke 12:49). This urgency is imperative to the theology of church growth.

But here we confront a credibility gap. We use urgent words, but do we *feel* urgent about them? This credibility gap is illustrated by an evangelical choir. Our choir recently sang "Springs of Living Water." I tapped my foot with the sopranos' lilting melody and the basses' thumped-out counterpoint. The arrangement was enjoyable and even spunky. Then the words penetrated my mind:

"I thirsted in a barren land of sin and shame." The well-fed altos didn't look thirsty. The sopranos were well-groomed, even a little arrogant. They didn't look as though they had been in a land of shame—more likely they had attended a Dale Carnegie course. I never heard capitalistic choristers sing so convincingly about desperation. They sang about rescuing the perishing, but few of them had ever been out on an evangelism call. They were concerned about breath control and hitting the accidental in the fourth bar correctly.

Growing churches are those which have been most successful in eliminating this credibility gap. Some Baptist Bible Fellowship churches are "notorious" in this way. Their theology in practice is as urgent as in profession. When they talk of men going to hell, they believe!

A theology for church growth will not preach more than it believes. Baptists berate Catholic traditions as superstitious and empty. But what of our insistence on evangelical terminology? Many churches demand theology of specific words. People without the faith of the nineteenth century must worship with nineteenth-century clichés. They will listen with superstitious awe to a dishonest Southern Baptist Convention evangelist (lately come from a day of filing his nails, fluffing his hair, and watching "As the World Turns") talk about the desperation of saving souls. I would rather hear an honest Episcopalian preach on Martin Heidegger.

We are phony when we reverence evangelism packaging. If the content doesn't match the wrapping, we don't have the theological consistency to grow churches. An honest liberal is at least not two-faced. Permit me a proverb for growing churches: Urgent is not as urgent says—urgent is as urgent does!

3. A Simple Theology

Simplicity and urgency are like horse and carriage, love and marriage. They go together. Let's go back to Mr. Smith's house. "Great Scott, Smitty, your house is on fire" is the urgent message. Do you add, "By the way, my wife wanted to know if you could come for pinochle Friday night"? Diversity is the enemy of urgency.

I remember calling for prayer requests one night. A man asked prayer for a friend. "What is the matter with your friend?" I asked. "Well," he said, "he just had a gall bladder attack." I thought that a rather urgent request. He went on, "But his attack was very bad since he has been a diabetic for years." I assured him that God could heal a diabetic victim of a gall bladder attack. "Still," he continued, "his advanced leukemia may complicate things if the doctors decide to operate." The urgency of the situation was ebbing. "The poor man," he went on, ."should do all right if he survives the heart attack he had on the way to the hospital." I barely suppressed a chuckle when we got to heart trouble. My compassion was drowned by diversity.

I usually find that urgent messages must be simple. We can be urgent about only one thing at a time. Any organization can grow with simple priorities. A peanut seller who sees peanuts as fundamental for human happiness may triple his sales overnight. If, however, he tries to sell peanuts and pipe wrenches with the same urgency, his success will be diffused. Every addition to his sales list will further obscure the urgency of his presentation.

Churches grow on the basis of one or two priorities—no more. The danger in the institutional church is little organizations that spring up which do not minister to the core concept: Camera Club, the Girls' Friendly Society, Boys' Brigade, Candy Stripers, etc. The simplistic theology of repentance thunders from the pulpit, but a new member is more readily approached to attend the Breakfast Club than to be saved.

Paul echoed the importance of simplicity: "And I, brethren, when I came to you, came not with excellency of speech or of wisdom, declaring unto you the testimony of God. For I determined not to know any thing among you, save Jesus Christ, and him crucified" (1 Cor. 2:1–2).

Jesus commended childlike simplicity (Matt. 18:3) and said

the significance of his life is hidden from the wise and revealed unto babes (Luke 10:21). Only when our eye is single can our body be filled with light (Matthew 6:22). Only when our theology and proclamation are single will the church body grow.

Here, then, is the theology of church growth: conservative, urgent, simple.

Conservative: "I . . . exhort you, that ye should earnestly contend for the faith which was once delivered unto the saints" (Jude 3).

Urgent: "Repent ye: for the kingdom of heaven is at hand . . . Prepare ye the way of the Lord . . . Whose fan is in his hand, and he will thoroughly purge his floor, and gather his wheat into the garner; but he will burn up the chaff with unquenchable fire" (Matt. 3:2–3,12).

Simple: "Preach the word" (2 Tim. 4:2).

Notes

1. John A. T. Robinson, *Honest to God* (Philadelphia: Westminster Press, 1963), p. 20.

2. Dean M. Kelley, *Why Conservative Churches Are Growing* (New York: Harper & Row, 1972), p. 8.

3. John R. Bisagno, *How to Build an Evangelistic Church* (Nashville: Broadman Press, 1971), p. 158.

4. Thomas Howard, *Christ the Tiger* (New York: J. B. Lippincott, 1967), p. 39.

5. David L. Mueller, *Karl Barth* (Waco: Word Books, 1972), p. 109.

6. Francis Schaeffer, *The Church at the End of the Twentieth Century* (Downers Grove: Inter-Varsity Press, 1970), p. 22.

9
The Christology of Church Growth

The church is owned by a Jew! He bought it two thousand years ago, though it is small and without business assets. The charter members were the dregs of humanity—detested by Romans and Jews alike. But on a dark Friday afternoon, the Lord handed over the purchase price. Then Christ, the sole owner of the church, got down to the basics.

For a few days he seemed to be an absentee landlord. Fire burned over obedience! Wind blew in gusty optimism. The ragamuffin church took to the streets. At the end of the day they were waterlogged from baptizing and hoarse from praising the Lord. An amazing parabola of church growth zoomed off the charts.

Softball was millenia ahead, and there were no pews to pack. It wasn't even "Kite Sunday." They had fixed their attention on one idea: It was not *their* church. Nor would it ever be. They bequeathed every later generation one inviolate principle of growth—the church belongs to Christ!

A specific Christology has always characterized the church. The church will not grow if owned by just any old Jesus. He must be that specific Christ born of Matthew's virgin, risen from Mark's tomb, ascended from Luke's mountain, and returning in splendor from John's crystal sea. Rudy Bultmann's Jesus is too fevered with *formgeschite* to grow churches. Tim Weber's Jesus is too stagestruck; Pere Teilhard's is unfinished; Pierre Burton's is angry. Joe Fletcher's Jesus cannot make moral decisions out of context.

Only the New Testament Christ is the agent of church growth. Uncertain redemption has no magnetism. The church is responsible for a clear word—the *Logos* daily becoming incarnate. Charles Merrill Smith pictures an uncertain Logos in his discussion of Arianism:

> Arius said he had the answer to the question as to whether Jesus was a god or a man. The answer, he said, was that in one sense Jesus is just like God, but in another sense he isn't. This, said Arius, on the one hand makes him not quite god, but on the other hand not quite man either. It was best to think of Jesus as a *tertium quid,* he said. Many people found this explanation very helpful.[1]

We must do better; we need a clear word. The Logos must be translated "Word" and not "Double-Talk."

Liberal pulpits pour forth life-killing, Christological doubletalk. But conservative churches bury their message in method and appear apathetic about Christology. The "How to Grow an Evangelistic Church" books often prefer kites to Christ.

I appreciate the rapid growth of evangelistic churches, but I am often stunned by their shallow philosophies. They are steeple-deep in charisma and methods. Listen to their Mardi Gras salesmanship, and you can tell that Christ is involved in the merchandising, along with other "fringe benefits." In one day you can leave the church with a coloring book, a kite, a doughnut, even a baptismal certificate, and an autographed picture of Brother Bob. Later it is clear that kites and coloring books are the most prized items, for baptismal certificates and pictures of Brother Bob litter the bus ramps.

Methods themselves may be a threat to evangelical Christology. Does Christ think it odd that Billy and Susie, who won the Samsonite luggage in a Sunday School contest, are yet unclear on their idea of honesty? Is the proverb for our age "Behind every great Sunday School there is a Shetland pony to be given as grand prize!"? Colossians 1:20 teaches that Christ made peace through his blood "to reconcile all things." Presentation of the interdepartmental trophy to the primary director in the methodological madness of the hyperevangelistic fellowship is unrelated to an evangelistic Christology.

The real tragedy is that the conservative superchurch and the small fellowship think in terms of statistical success, not a Christ-incarnated membership. Yet both are above the liberal fellowship. At least the components of an adequate Christology exist in some of these churches. They believe in a thoroughly New Testament Christ and maintain a surface loyalty to their presuppositions. In the liberal fellowship Christ is discredited and ultimately unable to save—salvation isn't within Jesus' human ability, and his divinity is gone.

What, then, should be our view of Christ? Well, to begin with, he must be a person. Gunther Bornkamm wants to make Christ a saving fact and reject him as a person. Gerhard Ebeling wants to reduce the personal Christ to a *Wortgeschehen*, a "word event." Rudolf Bultmann wants to make him an existential demand. I reject all these views. Christ is a person whom I must define in personal terms: the Builder and the Bridegroom. Let us pursue Christology in those terms.

The Builder

Christ is the Builder. This is the point of the mustard seed parable in Matthew 13:31–32. He is interested in building and growing the church. The harvest is a primary theme in the New Testament. Jesus referred to himself as *Lord of the harvest* (Matt. 9:38; Luke 10:2). Both John the Baptist and Christ spoke of their apocalypticism in terms of harvest. But the harvest and its fruits belong to the Lord of the harvest.

Again, the terms *Lord* and *Builder* are personal terms. This means that at the heart of the church is a person. Keith Miller in *The Becomers* says so-called plans of salvation have no validity when they become a scheme for saving others. The Bible knows no saving scheme, only a saving Lord. In pushing schemes we are likely to develop a *Christus ex machina,* a soteriology that is wholly cybernetic. Ultimately any "soul-saving" machine will fail. For the Builder of the church is not a mechanical ideology. He is a person.

I need to say clearly that I am talking here of the local church. The parable of the mustard seed causes thoughts of the universal church. But the universal church (the kingdom) only grows as the Lord of the church does his work in the separate corners. The universal church is millions strong and impersonal. The local church is dyspeptic and problem-ridden (see the First Baptist Church of Corinth in A.D. 47). It is easy to sing to the glorious Lord of the universal church, "Forward through the ages, In unbroken line" or "From Greenland's icy mountains, From India's coral strand." Back at Harmony Heights, the crowd is sparse and the communion service was more icy than Greenland's mountains.

The Lord knows that local building materials leave much to be desired. He began with Iscariot, Bar-jona, and the egoistic Boanerges. And while the difference between the church of the ages and Harmony Heights may be like the difference between a redwood and a bonsai, both churches have the same Lord and Master Builder.

If you doubt that Christ is the Builder, examine these basic passages: Acts 2:47—"And the *Lord* added to the church daily such as should be saved"; John 12:32—"And *I,* if *I* be lifted up from the earth, will draw all men unto me"; John 6:44—"No man can come unto me, except the Father which hath sent me draw him."

Jesus taught that he is the cornerstone (Matt. 21:42) in the superstructure of his church. While he is the chief stone, we are all "living" stones in that building (1 Pet. 2:4–6; Eph. 2:20–21).

The church is to remain loyal to its head (Col. 1:18). And the ministry of building is the ministry of search. Hear Don McGavran:

> Church growth follows where Christians show faithfulness in
> finding the lost. It is not enough to search for lost sheep.
> The Master Shepherd is not pleased with a token search; He
> wants His sheep found. . . . Church growth follows where
> the lost are not merely found but restored to normal life in
> the fold. . . . When Christians marching obediently under the
> Lord's command and filled with His compassion fold the wan-
> derers and feed the flock, then churches multiply.[2]

McGavran says that there are three kinds of church growth:
biological, transfer, and conversion.[3] *Biological growth* comes
from Christian parents, who usually "make Christians" out of
their offspring. Not always, as witnessed by the pop song,
"Poppa was a preacher, and Momma was a go-go girl!" But
usually.

However, a child brought up in the church may have very
little understanding of when being a "good little kid" turned
into being a real Christian. Their "Jesus Loves Me" Christology
was a warm beginning that never became a catharsis experience.
They were lullabied so often with "Amazing Grace" that they
never experienced it. This is not to say that they never accepted
grace. It is only to say that there was nothing "amazing" about
it; it was just "run of the mill" grace. Familiarity does not always
breed contempt, but it often breeds apathy.

The second kind of growth is *transfer growth*. I often call this
kind of growth ledger growth. As the old cliché has it, it majors
not on fishing but aquarium tending. It is paperwork Christianity:
credit and debit. McGavran sees this as maintenance membership
and not true kingdom growth. I would agree. While the angels
in heaven rejoice over one sinner who repents (Luke 15:7), they
have grown more used to those who come "on promise of a
letter."

The final kind of growth McGavran calls *conversion growth*. This
kind of growth adds branches to the mustard tree of Christ's
parable and is therefore the most important kind. "Conversion
growth is the only kind which really adds significantly to the

church . . . a church should not be satisfied until it is growing by conversion." [4]

Harold Fickett in echoing this theme says: "God is blessing our church because we are evangelistic. We are committed to the idea that men and women need to know Christ in a personal, viable way." [5] "Conversion growth rests squarely on New Testament Christology." [6]

Christology must be "desperate" as we have said. All universalisms, no matter how reasonable, are hostile to the Great Commission. The Christology of D. T. Niles is not a Christology of desperation. In the Lyman Beecher Lectures at Yale Divinity School he taught that all men were saved and that it was the task of the church to make their salvation known to them. In the name of tolerance this evangelistic world view has permeated the church. It is too void of dynamic to motivate the church to growth.

Conversion growth should be founded on serious repentance and costly grace. We are always trying to find an economic way to slip Christ in the side door of human experience so that no one need feel the exclusivist demands of witnessing. Charles Merrill Moore has described, tongue-in-cheek, this "cheap" grace by the words:

> We see another example of Gregory's administrative skill in correspondence, still extant, with Augustine. Gregory was a prolific giver of good advice on how to be an efficient administrator.
>
> Don't tear down the Anglo-Saxon pagan temples, he wrote to Augustine. Building costs are fierce. Turn the temples into Christian churches. Think of the money this will save!
>
> Don't abolish idol worship right off the bat, he counseled . . . after all, there isn't a great deal of difference between the worship of idols and the worship of saints. Pretty soon the English will hardly notice that they aren't worshipping their old idols anymore.[7]

Because of such a low Christology, we still call the greatest Christian holiday after the goddess of fertility and have wedded bunnies to the biblical theme.

Nothing is gained by cheapening Christology in the attempt to grow churches. Examples of it are limitless. In the typical Sunday School contest, the "Reds" are treating the "Blues" to a wiener roast. And some of the young converts, "Wienerlogged," turn to the eternal Savior, King of kings, and Lord of lords. Can a "wiener-bibber" be saved? Of course. But let us make sure that in the midst of the levity, he is not saved by mere propositions but by the mandatory encounter of the living Christ. There is little sin in pointing to Jesus with a charcoaled frankfurter, but as in all whims the real Christ must be seen, or the experience is spurious.

Emotionalism for its own sake obscures the real witness. Quite often Christ must be the key issue of witness and not secondary pulpit images. An evangelist once preached on hell to our congregation. He talked about fire victims he had met.

His message was full of grotesque images—a night walk through Nagasaki in September of 1945. Even though his fiery delivery said very little about Christ, there was much weeping.

Another evangelist of my acquaintance draws hordes of children to the altar. He often concludes his sermons with an illustration about a little boy who had been saved and became concerned for his parents. At his local Baptist church the child requested prayer for his father to be saved. His father was angered by his concern. As a result the little boy was beaten to death. At the end of the illustration and the sermon, the little boy was lying face down in a pool of blood in the bathroom. The sermon was, however, not "O positive" gore but "non-Christological." On the way home from church my young daughter said to me in the car, "Dad, that was surely too bad about the little boy lying face down in all that blood, wasn't it? His daddy must have been a mean man."

Once again Brother Brimstone emphasizes the principle that you do not have to be a liberal theologian to be guilty of a low Christology.

Mustard seed growth speaks basically of traditional evangelism. There are some traditions of dogma that do not change. The church is ever to enforce that which is unchangeable in its Christology. Hebrews 13:8 reminds us: "Jesus Christ [is] the same yesterday, and to day and for ever." Christ may not be "demythologized" and still be the Christ of the New Testament. We cannot be redeemed by clever nuances. The things we say of Christ must be the kinds of things that Simon Peter said about him, or our message is invalid.

There is another metaphor that describes the imperative newness in our Christology.

The Bridegroom

The marriage metaphor is built upon a message of newness. When marriage occurs, the bride and groom have a relationship which is new every morning. As conversion occurs, the Christ of the Caesars enters into the contemporary scene. The overwhelming impact of this new Christ is due to his profound relevancy in the life of the convert.

Christ is the bridegroom of his church. Only as he is allowed this marriage relationship is the church valid. But let us consider the tension between the two metaphors for just a moment. Traditional Christology can be a threat to the contemporary Christ. Christ the Builder and Christ the Bridegroom must be held in proper tension, or the Christology of the church becomes unstable.

In talking of the traditional Christ some seem to hold an unthinkable reverence for his antiquity. To these it seems sacrilegious to make him a real part of our culture. This flowing-robed, Oriental Jesus tends to get institutionalized and bound by a million Lilliputian views of himself. He is the Christ of the Sunday School print, the senior deacon Jesus. He is an ardent denominationalist and most loyal to those with the proper view of him. He is against change, always preferring that the piano sit on the right of the chancel. He loves convention but not innovation. He is decidely against wide ties, colored underwear, and long hair.

This traditional Christ paints posters and pickets his alter ego—the Superstar—the mod Messiah. This is the new Christ, the bridegroom-gone-too-far. He is too human. He identifies with all people down to the last neurotic. He is more like Nader than Nicodemus. He always lives far beyond the Gospels. He loves everything new: Evel Knievel and Transactional Analysis, rock gospels, and Esalen. He has never met King Herod but knows of the Harrad Experiment. He is generous to a fault yet never preaches or speaks restrictively. He just sits and bleeds with the world he loves but does not change, or ever desire it changed.

The best Christology balances these concepts: Christ the Builder and Christ the Bridegroom. Keeping Christ in the past will leave him powerless in our generation. On the other hand, imprisoning him in the contemporary scene leaves him without the biblical roots to say anything with authority.

The Builder suggests security and attachment to the beginning and continuity of the Christian faith, while the Bridegroom suggests newness and adventure. The Bridegroom principle feeds on anticipation and flexibility. While we may standardize the Christology of the Builder, we cannot standardize the Bridegroom Christology. This is the free Jesus, leading his church any way he wishes. The Bridegroom will never lead any two churches the same way, for he sees that no two churches are exactly alike. Robert Girard confessed to the utter transformation that occurred to his church when he made room for spiritual freedom:

The truth is, the Holy Spirit can be trusted to provide the church with all its needs to function as the New Testament reveals it should and can. True, he does these things in and through men; but he must be the one to do it! The hardest and most exciting thing that we are learning is the near-lost truth that the Holy Spirit can be trusted. He will build the church into a Living Body if we will simply stop trying to do His thing for Him—and let Him do it!

Everything that the Bible says about Him is true. And when He the Spirit does it, it is beautiful.

The pastors of Our Heritage made one drastic rule for our ministry as we began to try to get out of the way and let the Spirit do it.

"Anything in the church program that cannot be maintained without constant pastoral pressure on people to be involved should be allowed to die a sure and natural death!"

Three choirs died within two months! Along with the mid-week services and several committees. Within eighteen months, the Woman's Missionary Society was gone—we were down to one business meeting of any kind each month and another choir was about to bite the dust.[8]

For work in the fellowship the Bridegroom must be freed from the strictures of promotion and program.

The situation in the heavily programmed church is rather like the women of China who for centuries bound their feet to keep them small. The traditional church would like to grow, but it has so tied itself with strictures that it cannot. The machinery of evangelism and exegesis becomes enmeshed in the calendar and administrative agenda. Thus the freshness of innovation stagnates. The fellowship atrophies. The church designed to live on a millennial honeymoon with her groom becomes drab and perfunctory.

May the church dedicate itself to a relevant Christology where Christ is Lord of the whole church. Here's to value! Here's to faith and excitement! Here's to the Builder and Bridegroom!

Notes

1.   Charles Merrill Smith, *The Pearly Gates Syndicate* (New York: Doubleday and Company, Inc., 1971), p. 35.

2.   Donald McGavran, *Understanding Church Growth* (Grand Rapids: William B. Eerdmans, 1970), p. 15.

3.   Donald McGavran, *How to Grow a Church* (Grand Rapids: William B. Eerdmans, 1970), p. 87.

4.   McGavran, *Understanding Church Growth,* p. 59.

5.   Harold L. Fickett, *Hope for Your Church* (Glendale, California: Regal Press, 1972), p. 13.

6.   McGavran, *Understanding Church Growth,* p. 88.

7.   Smith, p. 72.

8.   Robert O. Girard, *Brethren, Hang Loose* (Grand Rapids: Zondervan Publishing House, 1972), pp. 72–73.

10
The Ecclesiology of Church Growth

"Church ain't shucks to the circus," said Tom Sawyer. He was right for a couple of reasons. I remember that as a child I wanted to run away and join the circus. On the other hand, I never wanted to run away and join the church. I went to a circus recently and was entranced. Even when I enjoy church services I feel no glitter, as I did in the circus. Now a part of my enjoyment was in expertise: aerial ballet, tiger fur sailing through flaming hoops, etc. Rarely do I see this expertise in church. I generally feel that Tom was right: "Church *ain't* shucks to the circus!"

I ask myself why the circus outdoes us. There are several reasons. The church is often guilty of maladministration. (The circus is always better scheduled and more performance oriented.) Let's bypass that for now.

One key to good ecclesiology is a proper definition of interparish relationships. Any distinction between administration and congregational relationships is artificial, to be sure. Scriptures show Christ's relationship to his church in the head and body imagery. Christ is seen as the head of the church, while the congregation (composed of both pastor and people) is the body (Eph. 1:22; 4:15; 5:23; Col. 1:18).

The New Testament word to describe the relationship within the fellowship would be *koinonia* (basically, partnership). Luke referred to Jesus' apostles as partners in the fishing business (5:10). Later the meaning was expanded to mean partners in God's business and even partners in suffering (1 Pet. 4:13; Phil. 3:10).

The relationship between pastor and congregation is usually illustrated as shepherd and sheep. The New Testament word for shepherd is *poimen;* the word for sheep is *probatos* (Matt. 10:16; 15:24; 25:33; 26:31). The word for taking care of the sheep becomes *poimaino* or "sheep-feeding" (John 21:16; Acts 20:28; 1 Pet. 5:1–2). This metaphor is definitely pastoral. But I do not agree that such imagery ill fits the technopolitan church of today. Seward Hiltner uses the Greek root to develop a pastoral ecclesiology. He calls his pastoral theology *poimenics* or shepherding.[1]

A hundred new images have been advanced to fit the contemporary urban scene better than *pastor. Player coach, sociological technician,* etc. have all in turn been suggested. But *pastor* as it comes through the Greek *episcopos,* the *overseer,* is still the best. Someone has suggested that the term *supervisor* literally means *overseer* and is a better term for pastor. It still seems a colder word and does not seem to have the empathy that tradition has built into the word *pastor.*

The ecclesiology of church growth is incumbent upon the word *pastor.* There are all types of pastoral styles. Each of them has definite strengths and weaknesses. Lyle Schaller demonstrates this in his book, *The Decision Makers.* Here is the monologue of a woman discussing the past three pastors of her church.

> Mrs. Adams said, "During the last twenty years we have had three pastors, Dr. Hanson, Pastor Anderson and now Ed Jackson."
> "The most important change that has taken place here at St. Luke's during the time I've been a member has been in the changing style of our ministerial leadership," Mrs. Adams went on. "This change in leadership style is reflected by terms we use in referring to or in addressing our pastor. Dr. Hanson had a very strong personality and he ran this parish. He was a very authoritarian HERR PASTOR type. You either did it the way Dr. Hanson wanted it done, or you got out. Occasion-

ally, he would ask individual members of the church council privately for their advice; but when my husband, who was on the church council for several years, left the house to go to a council meeting, he used to say, 'Well, tonight is the night we go to receive our marching orders for next month.' That's about the way it was, too.

"Dr. Hanson was followed in 1963 by Pastor Anderson, who was just the opposite type. When he graduated from seminary, he went to a small parish downstate and while there, he did additional graduate work in counseling. He was a wonderful pastor, a pretty fair preacher, and an awfully nice person. But if you asked him what time it was, he would ask what time you would like it to be, or why you asked.

"After Pastor Anderson resigned to go into the hospital chaplaincy, we called Ed Jackson. Ed is first of all a wonderful Christian individual. He is a person. Second, he is a warm, understanding and helpful pastor. Third, he knows how to be a leader and is willing to be an active leader. Fourth, he's a good manager." [2]

Of the three types of pastors, Ed Jackson is definitely our man in church growth. However, if you are prone to move from Ed to the next winning type, you must avoid pastor Anderson altogether and consider Dr. Hanson. Dr. Hanson seems to be the same kind of spiritual Fuehrer about whom was written the words:

The Rector is late,
He's forgotten the date,
So what can the faithful do now,
Poor things?

They'll sit in a pew
With nothing to do
And sing a selection of hymns,
Poor things! [3]

Is the domineering pastor the only one who can lead a church to grow? Of course not. But only the pastor with real leadership can organize a church and direct it in outreach and measurable growth.

I like the poetic question posed by Dr. Wendell Belew. Staring at Carthagenian ruins of an old cathedral he watched as,

> Dry leaves blew and swirled through what had been a baptistry.
>
> I long
>   would wonder why
>   some churches grow
>   and others die.[4]

It is an intriguing issue. But the answer to the question is closely related to the issue of pastoring. Why is it that some enthusiastic young man arrives on a church field and says with enthusiasm, "Jesus saves," and immediately rigor mortis sets in; and the church begins dying? On the other hand, some begin their calling in a most difficult place; and before you know it there's a thriving, growing church. The pastor lies at the fulcrum of the issue. If the pastor is "somehow" right, things "somehow" happen.

Elmer Towns, the Baptist researcher of church growth, accentuates this fact:

> Some pastors seem to have an "extra power" so that the masses are moved by their sermons; their requests are unquestionably obeyed by followers, people seem to empty their pocketbooks into the offering plate, and sinners almost run down the aisle at their invitation. . . . How can Jack Hyles build a church from 700 to 5,000 with over 50 adult professions each Sunday, yet a few miles away several fundamental pastors struggle with mediocrity? These struggling pastors serve the same God, have access to the same spiritual reserves and follow the same principles, yet one seemingly fails and the other is eminently successful . . . Dr. G. Beauchamp Vick, pastor of Temple Baptist

Church, Detroit, has said, "Some are 200 men, 1,500 men or 3,000." [5]

Exactly why there happen to be so many 200 men and so few 3,000 men, Elmer Towns does not say. But nearly everyone would have to see some wisdom in his statement.

The great variable of pastoral leadership is charisma. A prime case in point is John Bisagno. I believe Pastor Bisagno is an observable example of the kind of pastor whose charismatic leadership results in church growth. His own view of church leadership is this:

> The leadership of the pastor is a very delicate matter. There is a fine line between leadership and dictatorship. . . . As pastor, you should take hold. Assume leadership. You do not have to have a church vote on whether or not to have cocktails at the next Sunday School party, or whether to gamble the church funds on the Kentucky Derby. . . . If the deacons want to steal the evangelists' love offering to pay for the revival expenses, tell them to get lost and give the man his money. If you take it up for him, give it to him. . . . The church does not have to vote whether or not to steal a man's offering. People have no respect for a man who does not know where he is going. . . . They want leadership. . . . You do not have to ask for leadership. *If you have to ask for it, you do not have it. . . . When you have to start reminding them that you are the pastor, you no longer are!* . . . Leadership may often be wrong, but never in doubt. You do not always have to be right, but you do always have to be the pastor.[6]

Bisagno really lives up to his credo. He has built a great church. I have an admiration for such men who have been able to demonstrate this kind of venturesome obedience to the Spirit of God.

But the man who best speaks my ecclesiology of growth is Urban T. Holmes III, whom I believe is an Episcopalian. Mr. Holmes sees the church growth pastor as a sacramental person. Remember that the word *sacerdos* means priest. A priest is the point of rendezvous between spirit and flesh, omnipotence and struggle. Baptists in preaching the priesthood of the believer have often closed their eyes to the priesthood of the pastor. Only in recent years have I been able to face the word myself. I have only lately discovered the similarities between the pastoral and the priestly. We preachers hear less formal confessions and provide less liturgical "last rites." We break the communion bread, baptize, and pray in hospital rooms. Thus wittingly or not, Southern Baptist preachers become a kind of *sacerdos* and are generally viewed that way by their people. Like most of my Baptist brothers, I have been slow to accept my own life as the unsanctified "holy" ground upon which God and his people meet.

The sacrament as a word has been equally offensive to other evangelicals, too. The very idea that there can be a "rite through which grace is mediated" is odious to us. But I agree with Dr. Holmes III that, speaking genuinely and honestly, there are "persons through whom grace is mediated." While most of the so-called "charismatic" pastors of our day would decry the term "sacramental," it is nevertheless true that the grace—yes, even saving grace—of God has been mediated through their lives to a great many people. There are various levels of this mediation of grace. But the sacramental person through whom God draws men to himself on a widespread basis is able to be truly *sacerdotal* to a maximum number of people.

What then shall we do with the old outcry against the "personality cult" pastor? Or how shall we cut off the criticism that Brother Shazam is the winner of a good many dolts and parrots whose vocabulary is limited to "Amen, preach on." I think we shall have to struggle against envy and professional jealousy for those who have the charisma to build great churches. And if we are truly interested in church growth, we shall have to free up our structured ecclesiology to permit the philosophy of Holmes to become a working reality.

I do not see the church as measured by the names of the people on the parish register. I doubt that it has ever been, except in the minds of the clergy. Every Christian community has almost always been identified by its relation to its priest or pastor, *and we ought to acknowledge this openly* [italics mine]. Much worry has been expended over the "personality cult" in the church, but in fact this is what makes it all "go." Clergy are not technicians. They must be sacramental persons; people through whom is experienced the person of the church and of Christ. . . . This is not an argument for or against Apostolic succession: and it is certainly not a suggestion that "clergyman" is a word in the active voice and "layman" in the passive voice. It is simply to say that we acknowledge the sacramental person, the *sine qua non* of the cohesive Christian congregation, as the source of ministry.[7]

If we are to have growing churches, we will have to have pastors who are sacramental persons; and we will have to make room for them.

In a sense, it is not possible to shout down the truly sacramental pastor. The stones cry out in his defense. His people rise to defend him, with logic when they can gather it, with emotion when they cannot. His own reliance on God has furnished him with a napalm Calvinism that is fearsome to go against. It is possible to drive him from the convention with his entire church, but it is rarely possible to drive him from his pulpit.

The sacramental person must not be confused with the "successful pastor." The "successful pastor" may arrive at a prestigious pulpit through suave intrigue. He may dress nicely. He may "project." He may appear to "ooze" with charisma. But he is not a "sacrament" mediating grace from God—only his own grace. He will likely be what was called in eighteenth-century England "a fox-hunting parson." Harriet Beecher Stowe described these kinds of Puritan preachers so well one would think she had just come back from a contemporary urban ministerial alliance: "full-bottomed, powdered wig, full flowing coat with ample cuffs, (and) silver knee-and-show buckles." [8] Clearly, the "successful pastor" is a fox-hunter. He has sold out to middle-class value. He is captive to his own self-importance. He means well, but he is not to be feared.

Churchmen will have to face one other fact about the sacramental person. It will do not a whit's good to protest his intellectual content. If you feel the need to say that Paul Tillich is deeper than Jerry Falwell, forget it. We will not be convinced by your protest that "a college professor says more in three minutes than an evangelist does in a decade." We are not talking about the logical but the liminal. We are talking about the meeting of man and God on a personality. One more quote from Urban Holmes and I give him up. Holmes has suggested that the best model for a sacramental pastor might be the witch doctor:

> Theodore Roszak, in his book on this subject, makes an eloquent plea for us to look again at the meaning of magic. He continues by saying: "When we look more closely at the shaman, we discover that the contribution this exotic character has made to human culture is nearly inestimable. Indeed, the shaman might properly lay claim to being the culture hero *par excellence,* for through him creative forces that approach the superhuman seem to have been called into play." [9]
>
> He goes on to explain how the shaman, through the use of magic, opened man's imagination to realms of existence he never would have known otherwise. It is no wonder that a whole segment of our population are out looking for their 'guru.' As Roszak maintains, this need of people for new images of life confronts our anemic American religion with an undeniable challenge that pure rationalism cannot answer. Without pursuing to absurdity the notion of the shaman and his magic, it seems entirely possible to me that the charismatic quality he possessed, which marked him as a liminal man, is in fact what is needed in our ministry if we are to awaken people's imaginations to the possibilities of the future. I am not suggesting that we place in leadership roles actual or incipient psychotics. . . . But it is possible that we have made a fetish out of "normalcy." [10]

The church-growing pastor cannot be defined except in terms of liminal. The secrets of his sacrament are elusive. We may copy his style of ministry and yet never achieve his inwardness. The xeroxed photocopies fail.

The pointlessness of it all was pointed out by the publishing of a whimsical "Parish Rector Rating Chart." Part of the chart appears on page 109.

In thinking of your own pastor, please check a category. The list goes on, but the point is that the pastor who grows churches is definitely a "category 1" pastor. He is the Dalai Lama, admired, revered, loved, and defended. Even he could not tell you why. He would explain it in terms of the "unction" of God on his life. And that is as adequate an explanation as there is.

Remember, too, that the word "Christ" comes from a Greek word that means "the anointed One." And in every sense, he bears the "anointing" of God. While he would probably decry it, he does become the "Christ symbol" for his congregation. Every Sunday is "Palm Sunday." They wave their palms and stand in line to shake his hand. Whatever they intend to say at the back door, it comes out "hosanna." They give him his gifts on his birthday, anniversary, Veteran's Day, and the Day of the Great Pumpkin. He never enters the pulpit except he has come from the right hand of the Father.

Miracles accompany him wherever he walks. Men and women come out of sordid circumstances and cry out of their sins. They are born again. Joy, therefore, springs up around him. There is expectancy at the mention of his name. In the hospital room a withered old man intones, "He came today!" A ripple of excitement arises on visitation night: "Behold he, the pastor, stands at the door and knocks!"

And the congregation is supercharged on Sunday. There are static sparkles running along the pews. Fire unborn crackles around the pulpit. The deacons come in from the prayer room, taut with dry-cell amperage. The choir thunders the raw, bass kilowatts and coloratura electricity. Great Scott, man! Can you

My pastor—			
Leaps tall obstacles with a single bound	Must take a running start to leap over tall obstacles	Can leap over small obstacles only	Crashes into obstacles when attempting to jump over them	Cannot recognize obstacles at all
Is faster than a speeding bullet	Is as fast as a speeding bullet	Not quite as fast as a speeding bullet	Would you believe a short bullet	Usually wounds self with bullet
Is stronger than a herd of bulls	Is stronger than several bulls	Is stronger than one bull	Shoots the bull	Smells like a bull
Walks on water consistently	Walks on water in emergencies	Swims in water	Washes in water	Drinks water

stand the coming storm? The cables are damaged—the insula-
tion is ripped away, and the megavoltage lies bare and joyous.
Speak, trump of God, or we die!

Leave if you must. I will wait upon such a man. For while I
may not learn from him, upon his life I may meet my Father
in a moment of fire. He is the sacrament! And after all, what
did *you* go out to see—"a reed shaken with the wind?" (Matt.
11:7).

Notes

1. Seward Hiltner, *Preface to Pastoral Theology* (Nashville: Abingdon
Press, 1958), p. 69.

2. Lyle Schaller, *The Decision Makers* (Nashville: Abingdon Press,
1974), pp. 171–172.

3. John R. W. Stott, *One People* (Downers Grove: Inter-Varsity Press,
1968), p. 9.

4. Wendell Belew, *Churches and How They Grow* (Nashville: Broadman Press, 1971), p. 14.

5. Elmer L. Towns, *America's Fastest Growing Churches* (Nashville:
Impact Books, 1972), pp. 193–194.

6. John R. Bisagno, *How to Build an Evangelistic Church* (Nashville:
Broadman Press, 1971), pp. 17–20.

7. Urban T. Holmes III, *The Future Shape of Ministry* (New York:
Seabury Press, 1971), p. 229.

8. Ibid., p. 81.

9. Ibid., p. 246, as quoted from Theodore Roszak, *The Making of
a Counter-Culture* (New York: Doubleday and Company, Inc., 1969).

10. Ibid., pp. 246–247.

11
The Psychology of Church Growth: a Conversionist Psychology

Whatever the psychology of church growth is, it does not appear to be working too well. Lyle Schaller confronts us with the cold statistics of things as they are:

> Almost exactly half of the congregations in the United Presbyterian Church in the USA have fewer than 200 members. (In 1972 the smallest congregation in the UPCUSA had one member.) Approximately half of the congregations in the United Methodist Church have fewer than 150 members. Half of all churches in America have an average attendance at Sunday morning worship of fewer than 80, and a quarter average fewer than 40.[1]

Charles Merrill Smith accuses the contemporary church of what he calls a "Duesenberg Psychology":

> The trouble is that the church, except in rare instances, doesn't put on a very good show by today's standards. One can get a lot better music on his hi-fi. Speakers more entertaining and enlightening than most preachers are available at the flick of a dial. Fewer and fewer people care to drag themselves out of bed to sing hymns written from a pre-modern worldview and, apart from the nostalgia they create in some of us older types, have no particular merit.
>
> My conviction is that the churches, as they are now organized, have had it. They are like a 1932 Duesenberg. A 1932 Duesenberg was a fine automobile. It was, and still is for that matter, a handsome automobile. It was comfortable to ride in. Mechanically, it was way ahead of the times. One took pride

in being a Duesenberg owner. But they were expensive to
buy. The upkeep was horrendous. And they were awfully big.
Cheaper makes, smaller, better-suited to the purpose for which
a car is designed, drove the Duesenberg out of business.

A Duesenberg today is a status symbol, an expensive toy.

It seems to me, that the churches as we know them are
afflicted with the Duesenberg psychology. They assume that
somehow people can be persuaded to continue paying Duesenberg prices for their religion, even though the churches—while
costing a bundle—don't do the job for which they were designed anymore, at least not very well.

My suggestion is to let the people who want Duesenberg
religion, and are willing to pay for it, go right on playing with
their expensive Christian toy. After all, it's a free country, and
they can't hurt anybody very much. But please send a revelation
to some new Amos or Isaiah to call the community of faith
to its true vocation, which is best summed up, it strikes me,
in the traditional description of the Christian ministry as "a
cure of souls." [2]

This iniquity of the Duesenberg psychology was brought home
to me in a very real way a few years ago when my wife and I
happened to be in Brussels on Whitsunday. We attended St.
Michael's for mass. It was a major holiday, but few came to
church. We were present with some twenty to thirty other communicants in the cavernous cathedral. The dark and eerie Gothic
arches stretched into infinity behind us. But in spite of the very
few who looked on, no part of the Whitsunday pageant was
left out. The cardinal "swished" in like "Ruby Red-dress" and
"Latinnated." The liturgy was unchanged for four hundred
years: he did not forget his lines. There were a couple of guards-
men who preceded him to the chancel, complete with helmets
and medieval gaffs. It was definitely Duesenberg.

We have already established that the growing church feeds
on a conversionist psychology. Many of the psychologists of our
day and others disagree that the conversionist psychology is
best. William James and Erich Fromm were both critical of the

mental health of those who support conversionist religion. William James, in building his categories of "once born" and "twice born" religion, felt that "once born" was best. "Once born religion" is for those who had *real* inward peace. "Twice born religion" was bad in that it majored on *dependency* and *cultural conflict.*[3]

Erich Fromm made the same kinds of distinction between humanistic and authoritarian religion. Humanistic religion majored on man's goodness and autonomy. Authoritarian religion majored on man's depravity and consequent dependence.[4] Freud, Skinner, May, and Maslow would agree. Maslow has admittedly been engaged in the search for "peakers," and his search has been somewhat discouraging. In all of his "peaker-seeking," he has found very few "self-actualizers" and none under middle age. But he has been critical that a Christianity which is conversionist in psychology can produce any self-actualization. As a matter of fact, he had likened conversionist dialogue to "nonpeakers talking to nonpeakers about peak experience." [5]

The dominant and contemporary Transactional Analysis does not seem to be the friend of the conversionist psychology. It is difficult to balance "I'm OK, You're OK" with the conversionist doctrine of human depravity. But we have a friend in psychology, Karl Menninger, who is convinced that mental health and moral health sleep close together. The numerous passages of the Bible upon which the conversionist psychology depend are support for Menninger. To speak of our "OK-ness" in the face of Isaiah 53:6 or Romans 3:23 is to be guilty of what Menninger would call the "bluebird on the dung-heap." [6] It is morality by pretense.

The Scriptures teach that man is evil and in need of grace. His sin needs to be confronted and confessed. His damnation cannot be concealed by his pretended sinlessness. Karl Menninger confronts this need in the poem by Elmer F. Suderman:

Here they are
my pampered flamboyants,

status spoiled, who bring
with exquisite zing
their souls spick and span
protected by Ban . . .
exchanging at my call
with no effort at all . . .
theology for television.

There they go
my in-crowd
my soft-skinned crowd,
my suntanned, so-so
elegant, swellegant,
natty, delectable,
suave, cool, adorable
DAMNED! [7]

Churches can grow only if they face the sinfulness of their environment. If sin is not real, then conversion has no purpose. Remember that conversion is part repentance and part faith. If there is no sin, then repentance is absurd and meaningless, and faith is impossible.

This is a day when the conversionist view may be suffering because the church has (unwittingly perhaps) adopted a more congratulatory psychology and dismissed its denunciatory doctrine of sin. But some churches are still preaching grace for guilt and salvation from sin.

Motivational Psychology:

There are some obvious ways that conversionist psychology is related to a motivational psychology. Conversion is usually presented upon the basis of a reward-and-punishment model. "If you do not repent, you will perish" (Luke 13:3; John 3:36; 3:18, author's paraphrase). But while the motivation factor in conversion could be discussed at length, let us turn our attention to other less "theological" aspects of the psychology of motivation in church growth.

The psychodynamics of motivating church members to make the church grow have usually been carrot-and-stick tactics. Motivation would be according to McGregor's Theory-X view that a great deal of direction is required since the average church member is not very creative and is not a self-starter. This is what Harry Levinson refers to as the "Great Jackass Fallacy." The laymen in some fast growing situations have been assumed to be dolts only capable of achieving a growing church as they are manipulated by a highly autocratic pastor.

In such situations, guilt becomes a primary motive. "Why is the Youth Department down to 275 this week? What is the matter, Youth workers? Look at what the Children's workers did." Sometimes the guilt is engendered by a series of spiritualizations: "If you love the Lord, you'll get out this Saturday afternoon and make sure that Rally Sunday is a record day." There are many aspects to the motivational psychology that operates in a growing church, but let us look at some specific aspects of it.

1. It Is a Psychology of Survival

Don Metz discusses the formal goals and the survival goals of new congregations.[8] The survival goals relate to evangelism and the building of the building. Dr. James Kennedy of the Coral Ridge Presbyterian Church best illustrates the nature of survival goals. Before Dr. Kennedy became a personal evangelist, he confessed that he pastored a church that had "grown" from thirty-eight to nineteen under his leadership. He realized that unless something was done soon, there would be no church. Evangelism became the hope of his church; and within a few years, the church had become one of the largest in the nation.

The thought of extinction can become a high source of motivation in church growth. Many pulpit committees are looking for a miracle worker to resurrect their dying churches. In sheer

desperation, laymen have followed all kinds of visitation programs in a frantic attempt at survival.

2. It Is a Product-Oriented Psychology

A psychology professor conducted an experiment to prove a
point about work. He hired a man to hit a log with the reverse
side of an axe. The man was told that he would be paid twice
the amount he normally made. The fellow lasted half a day.
He gave it up, explaining, "I have to see the chips fly."

In church growth also there has to be a measurable, countable
product. Statistics become all-important as motivators. They are
exchanged at the coffee urn in preachers' get-togethers. They
are laid before the congregation, sometimes with congratula-
tions—other times in reprimand.

A part of the product for the layman is the recognition and
title that he receives. He may be a "bus pastor" or a "departmen-
tal director." But the psychology is often materialistic in the
evangelistic "superchurch." For the hard worker, there are all
kinds of fringe benefits.

"Look, Mommy, I won a transistor radio for perfect attendance!"

"Don't bother Mommy now, darling. I've got to make forty
revival calls and try to win that weekend in Bermuda."

Perhaps a good bit of the product is mere recognition in a
day of anonymity. Here, before the throng, the eight-to-five as-
sembly liner is given an award. "Bus 32 wins the route of the
week!" "The Intermediates win the attendance banner!" "Mr.
Jones gets the picture of Jesus painted by Mrs. Smith." Suddenly
the forgotten machinist is a real man, respected for "making
the chips fly" in his church. And he has a photograph of himself
with the pastor, the number 1 hero of his life.

Some of this product psychology sounds like this:

"A million more in '54"—an SBC motto of twenty years ago.

"We shall average 1501 before we are done with '71"—Bible
Baptist Church in Savannah, Georgia.[9]

"If we make much of Jesus, He will make much of us." [10]

> Dr. John Rawlings, in Cincinnati, put a Santa Claus suit on
> every bus driver and had one of the largest attendances on
> the buses, resulting in one of the largest crowds on Christmas
> when attendance usually dropped. Pastor Dixon, believing in
> one-upmanship, put Santa Claus suits on his bus drivers every
> Sunday in December and broke a month-long record. . . .
> However, bus drivers who were in the choir were not allowed
> to wear their Santa Claus suits into the choir.[11]

"Goldfish Sunday was also a big Sunday." [12]

Such is the nature of motivational psychology.

3. The Fear of the Beast

The fear of "the beast" is another motivator in the growing
church. Exactly what the beast is may vary from motivational
system to motivational system. But it is always something to
be feared. Bertrand Russell is reported to have said that you
don't have to have a God to succeed, but you must have a devil.
His is the truism that we are more drawn to alliances by common
hatreds than by common loves. We are all a little like Ralph
and Piggy and Samneric in *Lord of the Flies.* Our unity becomes
fierce when we are pursued by our most dreaded foe.

The hated beast of some thriving evangelical fellowships may
be the National Council of Churches, liberal seminaries, psychia-
trists, lottery advocates, Communists, or acid rock. If the church
is growing rapidly, some time is usually spent attacking the beast.
The beast will usually be defined frequently before the congregation. The pastor of the flock will lash out regularly at the dreaded
beast, for he is always the enemy of church growth. He is against
the virgin birth of Christ and reads *Playboy* magazine as he smokes

marijuana on the way back from "art" theaters: "Well, you got trouble, my friend, right here in Baptist City, with a capital 'T' and that rhymes with 'B', and that stands for the beast."

Generally the beast is an *id*, not a person. We are to love sinners but hate their sin. We don't really "hate" Billy Graham; we just can't have "fellowship" with him because he "fellowships with modernists." I once read a sermon on the "filthy, dirty, rotten, modern dance." I knew that such dances were to be eschewed by truly born again people; after all, you can "never find a dancing foot and a praying knee on the same leg." But I did not know the beast was so hard to track.

Remember Brother Fred Chicken, who could preach a stirring sermon on the evils of dancing in Baptist colleges and then go home to an old Ginger Rogers-Fred Astaire movie? But it is immoral to try and defend the beast. Logic is impossible. Thomas Howard describes the elusive nature of the beast in *Christ the Tiger:*

> If you ask someone what he thinks of when he thinks of a fundamentalist, he will probably tell you that it is a person who does not smoke or drink or gamble or go to the theater. . . . If the taboos had been understood as matters of taste or inclination or health, no one could argue. But they were given a divine authority. . . . I knew people, for instance, who in the name of religion had to spend time deciding between the Beatles and the Lettermen as to which group could be listened to without sin. They did not allow music if that music had been heard on a film, and they objected to long, straight hair on girls, if that was the fashion of the moment, and to short hair, if that was the fashion. I spent some time once with another, equally earnest group that was vigorously aware of the number of inches between the sleeve and wrist, and between the hemline and the floor. They, too, were inclined to regard hair styles as having moral significance and saw a bun as probably the most Godly arrangement. . . . Another used clear fingernail polish, but not colored. . . . The idea

was that all sorts of bad women, from Jezebel to Maria Theresa and Clara Bow, had used make-up, and if one were to avoid the appearance of evil, one did not use paints. I remember hearing one girl fling in the teeth of a less zealous girl, 'I never use a thing on my face.' At the time, I agreed with her doctrine, but I had misgivings about her face as an example of divine loveliness.[13]

The beast is the encroachment of ghastly worldliness. It is to be screamed at from the pulpit. Thomas Howard had tried on occasion to see the beast with logic:

> "If it was objected that movies feed bad thoughts into people's minds, shall we then place books under the interdict?"
>
> "Oh, no—there are good books, so we can't eliminate all books."
>
> "Are there no good films?"
>
> "Well, yes, but if you start allowing some, you've let down the barrier. . . ."
>
> "Are they not doing that with books already?"
>
> "Possibly. . . ."
>
> "Well, hadn't we better interdict books then?"
>
> "Well, you see, movies represent an industry."
>
> "Books don't?"
>
> "How?"
>
> "The actors lead such bad lives."
>
> "Do they?"
>
> "Yes."
>
> "All of them?"
>
> "Most of them."
>
> "Do authors and publishers lead good lives?"
>
> "I don't suppose they do."
>
> "Well, we had better interdict books . . ."
>
> "No, you can't do that. Books are an individual matter. You can't keep people from reading Dickens just because they might then read *Fanny Hill* or *Naked Lunch.*"[14]
>
> "The idea was that, what with the marital intricacies of Beverly Hills and one thing and another, inasmuch as you paid

$1.00 for a movie, you contributed toward someone's Baccha-
nalia out there. This kind of caution did not apply, on the
other hand, to other forms of entertainment. You did not ask
about the extracurricular sexual irregularities of the clowns
and acrobats and elephant keepers when you paid your money
at the circus gate." [15]

If Dean Kelley is to be believed, the fear of the beast is a
powerful motivator in the psychology of church growth. The
churches which are growing, says Kelley,

are not "reasonable," they are not "tolerant," they are not
ecumenical, they are not "relevant." Quite the contrary! They
often refuse to recognize the validity of other churches' teachings. . . . It is ironic that the religious groups which persist
in such "unreasonable" and "unsociable" behaviour should
be flourishing, which the more "reasonable" and "sociable"
bodies are not.[16]

A part of the beast is the number of translations of the Bible.
In preaching in one of the "fastest-growing churches in America," I was told (as I carried my *New American Standard Bible* into
the pulpit), "We don't use that Bible in this church, son." One
woman I heard about in Nebraska feared the best of new translations so badly she argued with our missionary, "I trust the King
James so completely that if I had all of the original manuscripts
in my hand, I would not hesitate to throw them into the fire
and just go right on depending on my King James." One can
be thankful she was not the discoverer of Qumran.

The beast must always be met with force. There is only one
way to handle *Jesus Christ Superstar,* Malcolm Boyd, Southern Baptist liberalism, the National Council of Churches, William Peter
Blatty, Bette Midler, Angela Davis, Billy Graham, Anton LaVey,
C. S. Lewis, Norman Peale, Sun Myung Moon, Lassie, Captain
Crunch, and *The New English Bible*—"Abstain from all appearance
of evil!" (1 Thess. 5:22).

Just how much the beast is the motivator in the new evangelicalism may be witnessed in the straightforward testimony of Betty Elliot in her stunning little volume *The Liberty of Obedience*. She tells how she finally did manage to infiltrate the Auca culture after her husband's martyrdom. When many of the Indians were coming to Christ, she felt compelled to strengthen them against the beast. She wanted to tell them, "You must not tango. You must despise cinerama. You must not wear makeup. You must not smoke." The truth of the matter was that she was in a culture where the beast as she knew it did not exist. The nearest movie was hundreds of miles away in Quito. They couldn't imagine pari-mutuel betting or poker. No makeup! No nothing! Without a beast, she came to the startling discovery that Christianity is Christ. It does not exist over against a world of negative values. It does not even depend upon those negative values for its existence. It is the inner presence of Christ . . . . the joy of obedience in liberty.

4. Psychology of Concurrence Seeking

Now that we have looked at both the positive and negative forms of motivational psychology, let us look at one more aspect in the psychology of church growth. Concurrence seeking is usually titled "glorious fellowship." An article in *Psychology Today* some years ago defined concurrence seeking as *groupthink:*

> The symptoms of groupthink arise when the members of decision-making groups become motivated to avoid being too harsh in their judgments of their leaders' or their colleagues' ideas. They adopt a soft line of criticism, even in their own thinking. At their meetings, all the members are amiable and seek complete concurrence on every important issue, with no conflict to spoil the cozy, "we feeling." [17]

Many of the weaknesses of this psychology have been demonstrated by the pastors of the great churches. They have tended to gather around them those who are energetic and enthusiastic but who are more known for their cordial endorsement than their individual criticism of the program.

The error of concurrence-seeking psychology is probably observable in the various bouts of prominent pastors with the Securities and Exchange Commission. One wonders how often the Mid-Cities Baptist Church in New Orleans had sweeping rallies of affirmation for the staff right up to the moment of embarrassing insolvency.

One thing is for sure: When concurrence seeking reaches its zenith, then any criticism, no matter how valid, becomes a part of the beast. One of these super pastors may say something worth hearing about himself as a leader of concurrence when he says: "This reminds me of the story of the pastor who said that he put on a membership drive and drove out fifteen. Whenever an individual wants to put himself in the position of church dictator, the best thing that can happen is for that individual to go." [18] One would agree that any person who seeks to usurp the position of the pastor is a danger to the flock. However, the sensitive pastor should be open to valuable criticism when it is redemptive, even if it does jangle the "we feeling" of the leadership.

But in the name of Christian fellowship, there is a heavy motivational pressure applied to be together in all things. And *most* churches that are growing by what McGavran calls "conversion growth" rather than "transfer growth" have a high susceptibility to groupthink. These churches are filled with welcome and camaraderie. They say in every service, "Welcome to our congeniality. If you believe this is the best church in the world, say 'Amen!' But if you believe it is not in the top ten, watch out! We don't accept that kind of demonic pessimism even from the bus-greasers."

Thus go most of the public services, rich in conversion, rich in motivation, and rich in concurrence. But in contrasting this kind of psychological togetherness with the usual congregational grudges of the nongrowing church, I am prone to say that the "togetherness syndrome" with all of its excesses is best. There is something good about seeking togetherness, even in the face of its excesses. Having had both well-meaning critics and blind supporters, I must confess that I like the supporters best. The critics have sometimes been worth hearing, but their abrasive advice ruffled the fellowship and often polarized it.

I do know that when the concurrence level is high, the psychology of motivation is productive. I like the feeling that the old mustard tree is adding branches and the kingdom is gathering Christ's elect. And if our approach is shallow and lacks the depth of the great humanitarian and theological movements of history, I still prefer it to all else.

While I do not always like the "carnival atmosphere" that my own motivational psychology pursues, I do like the color and the bangles and the lights.

Given my disenchantment with inflation and Watergate and my chances for carcinoma or phlebitis, what's wrong with a little carnival? Maybe here and there the joy *is* authentic, and we are not just smiling through our acid indigestion. There are real conversions! The glittering "go-go" is strictly Matthew 28. There will be surprises and music and excitement and for someone, a brass ring—all at the direction of the Spirit. And under his direction all motivation is authentic. Joy baptizes worship and life itself as he directs. I pray such excitement may characterize my own work. I pray it may be said of Omaha as it was of Samaria: "There was great joy in that city" (Acts 8:8). "And the Lord added to the church daily such as should be saved" (Acts 2:47).

Notes

1.   Lyle E. Schaller, *The Decision Makers* (Nashville: Abingdon Press, 1974), p. 61.

2.   Charles Merrill Smith, *How to Talk to God When You Aren't Feeling Religious* (Waco: Word Books, 1971), pp. 44–46.

3. William James, *Varieties of Religious Experience* (New York: Collier Books, 1971), p. 79.

4. Erich Fromm, *Psychoanalysis and Religion* (New York: Bantam Books, 1972), p. 34 f.

5. Abraham Maslow, *Religions, Values, and Peak Experiences* (New York: Viking Press, 1970), p. 24.

6. Karl Menninger, *Whatever Became of Sin?* (New York: Hawthorne Books, 1973), pp. 189–221.

7. Ibid., pp. 201–202.

8. Donald L. Metz, *New Congregations* (Philadelphia: Westminster Press, 1967), p. 54 f.

9. Elmer L. Towns, *America's Fastest Growing Churches* (Nashville: Impact Books, 1972), p. 131.

10. Ibid., p. 99.

11. Ibid., p. 64.

12. Ibid., p. 65.

13. Thomas Howard, *Christ the Tiger* (New York: J. B. Lippincott, 1967), pp. 84–85.

14. Ibid., pp. 88–89.

15. Ibid., p. 89.

16. Dean M. Kelley, *Why Conservative Churches Are Growing* (New York: Harper & Row, 1972), pp. 25–26.

17. Irving L. Janis, "Groupthink!" *Psychology Today* (November 1971), p. 43.

18. Harold L. Fickett, *Hope for Your Church* (Glendale, California: Regal Press, 1972), p. 2.

12
The Sociology of Church Growth

There are a great many things that could be said under this heading, but I would like to try and relate the issue of church growth to two things: (1) a view of man and (2) the sociological cycle of church growth. It is difficult to separate our view of Christ and our sociology. If we see man as a culturally endangered being, suffering from the larger and general inhumanity of the race, then most probably Jesus will be a kind of "incarnate sociologist." If we see man as a fallen, spiritual being, then Jesus becomes a more "docetic spirit" of salvation. If these categories seem unreal, perhaps we need to whet our understanding with evidence.

Church Growth and a View of Man

Joe Darion has his Man of La Mancha say that he is a country gentleman. No longer young, he still hopes to make a better world than dullards ever dream of. He constructs a world where evil does not bring profit while virtue fails. He lays down his "burden of sanity" to become a knight-errant. And off he goes to roam the world, to right every error as Don Quixote de la Mancha. The Man of La Mancha is a kind of messiah. He is a mystic and visionary, a Castilian sociologist. He concludes that the worst madness of all is to "see life as it is and not as it should be."

The view of Christ which is hardest on church growth is to see the Man of Nazareth as a Semitic sociologist, a knight-errant, who promises to right all wrongs. This "social-worker Savior" was Jesus to Father Groppe, and "loved" best in the theater of injustice. He never gets near WASP churches or the Baptist Bible Fellowship churches. In contempt, he drove by Bob Jones University on his way from Selma to the D.C. Freedom Rally. He seeks justice for the braceros, the amnesty-seekers, the free-speechers. He weeps for the miners in Appalachia, the American Indian Movement, the Soviet Jews, the ghetto blacks, and the shambled low-rise architectural abortions of Housing and Urban Development.

He is the ill-defined Christ of aching protoplasm. He is contemporary but often mythological, mostly symbol. He has risen out of liberal theology, which rejected his virgin birth from Mary of Nazareth and sadly opted for his parthenogenesis out of the existentialist milieu. In his most extreme image, this Christ does not grow churches; he doesn't even attend. He, like Marcion of old, has torn away all of the New Testament record except Matthew 25. He is so humanitarian that he will not even talk of God.

Often he looks beautiful—like the time when he stopped by Biafra on his weary way to Bangladesh. But much of the time his concerns have been small and even absurd. We want to say to him, "Physician, heal thyself!" It is written of one such crusade:

> This month of October has been designated Diabetes Detection Month, and the rector, himself a diabetic, offers this service to anyone who desires it. Just follow this procedure:
> 1. Collect a specimen of urine in a clean bottle and attach your name firmly by tape to this bottle.
> 2. Bring me the specimen and I will run the sugar test and report to you what I find. . . .
> Diabetes is an insidious disease and can cause serious trouble if it is present and undetected. So do not take a chance— the test will cost you nothing and I will be happy to be of service.[1]

But whatever this sort of humanitarianism accomplishes, it will not grow churches. This surgeon-general Savior is too much surgeon general and too little Savior to get excited about Sunday School buses or James Kennedy.

What, then, is the view of man that grows churches? Man must be seen as hopelessly lost in his sins (Rom. 5:6). He is a condemned creature (John 3:18). He will perish if he does not repent (Luke 13:3). He will be tormented forever if he does not turn to Christ (Rev. 20:11). It is precisely at this point that liberal theology is not a theology of growth but of death. In my own understanding, Barthian theology is liberal. As we have said, Barth returned us to a kind of orthodoxy but not to the desperation of the New Testament idiom. Two quotes, I think, will demonstrate this: "God's righteousness effects man's salvation—not his damnation. It is a merciful righteousness." [2] Secondly, on election, Barth taught: "This choice of the Godless man is void . . . . he belongs eternally to Jesus Christ and therefore is not rejected, but elected by God." [3]

The implication of these two quotes is obvious. Man is incapable of being damned even if he is Godless. While it might be argued that few evangelists would follow Barth all the way, the extent of this kind of universal soteriology, I believe, does prevail among many evangelists.

In such a view of man, the desperation is gone. The view of man that grows churches sticks to the more desperate biblical view. Some twenty-four times in the New Testament Jesus called himself *Savior* or at least allowed others to refer to him with this desperate term. Some fifteen times in the New Testament the term *perishing* is used of those who fail to believe. Six times in the New Testament the unbelievers are referred to as *lost.* A series of concordance references on the word *damned* or *damnation* offers this chilling evidence of desperation: "Woe unto you scribes . . . ye shall receive the greater damnation" (Matt. 23:14). "Ye serpents . . . how can you escape the damnation of hell?" (Matt. 23:33). "But he that shall blaspheme against the Holy Ghost . . . is in danger of eternal damnation" (Mark 3:29). "And shall come forth . . . they that have done evil unto the resurrection of damnation" (John 5:29). "Having damnation, because they have cast off their first faith" (1 Tim. 5:12). "Whose judgment . . . lingereth not, and their damnation slumbereth not" (2 Pet. 2:3). This is a partial list, but enough to leave us with the haunting desperation of the Bible's view of man.

Evangelism is inherent in this biblical view of man. A Union Theological Seminary graduate would look at a bracero and see a cheated man and the culprit of economic injustice: A Bob Jones grad would see him as spiritually destitute. The former would picket San Joaquin; the latter would witness from the gospel of San Juan. And it does no good to cry for a middle ground: may we not both witness and picket? Usually there is no hope for the middle of the road. The Union grad has an anemic Jesus, the "BJ-er" an anemic social concern. But given the same start, all other things equal, the "BJ-er" would be far more likely to succeed in building a church among the deprived than the liberal seminarian.

I am prone to agree with Urban Holmes again that the evangelical sees Christ as specifically human, in fact, the *true humanum*. Can we liberate man by altering the various cultural and economic structures and strictures? I do not think so. Man is liberated by affording him a model of all that might be if he were able to clearly visualize the most noble existence of himself. It is speaking to this possibility of conversion that Holmes says:

> *The task of the church is to provide a transcendent image of man!*
> Therefore, it is not enough to be a prophet. Evangelism is the first requirement, no matter how distasteful this may seem. . . . The church *qua* Church has only one thing to give the world—an image of God's purpose in creating man and the means of attaining it—namely, Christ. People who call themselves Christian may do other things, but it is not Christian ministry. Prophecy requires as its *major premise* that God has

revealed the true *humanum* in Christ. This lies at the heart of
Ivan Illich's repeated axiom: "The task of the church is not
to 'socialize' but to 'evangelize.' " [4]

To further demonstrate his point, Holmes quotes from
Tolstoy:

> The less efficient the church is as a power, the more effective
> she can be as a celebrant of the mystery. This statement, if
> understood, is resented equally by the hierarch who wants
> to justify collections by increasing his service to the poor, and
> by the rebel priest who wants to use his collar as an attractive
> banner in agitation. In my mind both symbolize obstacles to
> the specific function of the church: the communication of the
> Gospel.[5]

What I think Tolstoy means here, that social concern may
be an obstacle to the gospel, was expressed in Doestoevsky's
warning that ardent humanitarianism is really atheism in dis-
guise. Jesus warned us against this kind of anthropocentric concern when he chided the socially concerned Judas: "Ye have
the poor always with you." Jesus goes on to make a plea for
the exaltation of himself: "but me ye have not always" (Matt.
26:11).

To visualize it thus is the best. Then John 3:14 becomes not
an evangelistic presupposition for a Southern evangelist. It becomes a sociological tenet: "As Moses lifted up the serpent in
the wilderness, even so must the Son of man be lifted up."
This tenet assumes that every strata of culture, from the pariah
to the elite, is only saved from temporary meaninglessness and
eternal damnation as he catches sight of what it means to be
truly man.

The innocent Adam is the *true humanum,* man created as God
intended man to be. Man can return to this complete humanity
only as he is saved from his fallenness by the power of the
cross. Purely sociological salvation has some merit, of course,
but it is woefully incomplete. Can a solving of economic injustice

bring a bracero to this *true humanum?* It cannot! The believer, then, does have sociological obligations; but the greater of his obligations are soteriological. Only those who have a strong obligation to evangelism have a proper view of man. And only those with such a desperate view of man have a philosophy adequate to grow churches.

The evangelical has often been remiss in understanding his obligation for a social conscience. Rauschenbusch told about the Canadian dairyman who picked up his milk cans and found them plastered with large red labels, indicating that they had found traces of manure in his milk. These red labels irritated the farmer; and he swore an oath, a "worldly oath." He was overheard by a fellow church member; and he was hailed in before his church and excluded from the congregation. "Not," as Rauschenbusch pointed out, "for introducing cow dung into the intestines of babies, but for expressing his belief in the damnation of the wicked in a non-theological way." [6]

But correcting such situations is not the gospel. Sanitary dairymen have not arrived at this *true humanum*. If that were so, the Pure Food and Drug Administration could bring in the Kingdom. Is this to say that Ralph Nader is not interested in the *true humanum?* I think not. Nor is it to say that sociological apathy is ever excusable. We do have the obligation to pry the present globe as far as we can in the direction of utopia. But we are to do it with the clear understanding that man has been barred from Eden by his sinfulness. He may bang at the gates of Paradise but never return. We cannot build a sociological Eden on sinfulness. The old cliché is true: We cannot make a good omelet from bad eggs.

But I find some biblical and social variance in one of America's truly great preachers when he says: "One of the latest theological jags is that we must make the gospel relevant. That, my friend, is a lot of baloney. It is not our job to make the gospel relevant. Ours is to preach it. The Holy Spirit . . . makes it relevant." [7]

This kind of statement seems to me to be against the spirit

of Scriptures. Remember that Moses was interested in the abolition of slavery, a social issue. Amos was interested in economic justice, a social issue. Paul was at least opposed to some forms of civil disobedience (Rom. 13:1). Is it possible to say that the sermons of Martin Luther King are as valid as those of John Rice? How about Lord Shaftesbury? Or Charles Finney, who hid runaway slaves in a spirit of compassion and civil disobedience?

If we heard Martin Luther King right, he was saying in eloquent Alabama Hebrew, "Let my people go." If Shaftesbury could keep the four-year-olds out of the mines, he must have been from God, and his doctrine must be important. If Nader gets a buzzer on my seat belt and I live through a hundred thousand miles of freeway travel, then I am willing to concede his calling and the importance of it. And every once in a while there is a William Booth or a Robert Raines who puts social concern and Christian concern together for me. Somewhere there is a Jimmy Allen whose gospel has social content and yet comes to a Christ accepting at one time both eternal life and a pair of shoes.

But the view of man which will grow churches will always see man first as a spiritual being. John Bisagno may oversimplify; but he is, in general, laying down the sociology for church growth when he says:

> The priority of evangelism over social action must be clearly established. . . . When a man is saved, ideally many things happen. He may restore stolen property, thus help balance the economy. He will certainly work harder and be more honest at his job when helping to earn his salary and helping to stabilize inflation. He will keep a neater yard, empty trash properly, refrain from dumping crude oil into the lakes, and burning down the forests. A Christian is good for ecology. . . . He will love his neighbor regardless of race, color, or creed. Why? Because the preacher preached on ecology and race relations? Because he marched in a parade? No. Not at all. Because he is saved. He is a new creation. A new creature in Jesus Christ.

Only a fool would say that winning men to Christ is not a
priority and does not possess a total and absolute involvement,
the solution to social matters.[8]

This is an oversimplification, as has been said. I have been
a Christian for many years, and I have not kept a neater yard
than the leading atheist on my block. I also do not empty my
trash properly. The priority of evangelism is no cure-all for solving social problems. It will have to be accompanied by education
as well as cultural growth. But the priority of evangelism is
correct.

The Sociological Cycle of Church Growth

The year 1972 saw the publication of two books. While these
books issued from widely different backgrounds, they reinforced
each other on the subject of church growth. The first of the
books, *Why Conservative Churches Are Growing*, was written by Dean
M. Kelley, a former Methodist pastor and the director for the
Civil and Religious Liberty of the National Council of Churches.
The second book, *America's Fastest Growing Churches*, was written
by Elmer L. Towns and spends the first three-fourths in giving
a blow-by-blow account of the Baptist Bible Fellowship churches
and how they were growing. However, it is only the last fourth
of Towns' book that justifies the price of the book.

Towns is not completely original in suggesting what he called
"the sociological cycle of church growth." David Moberg, a
church sociologist from Marquette University, talked about such
a cycle where cults originate, develop into sects, change to denominations, and then emerge as churches. Ernst Troeltsch, the
German philosopher-sociologist, also talked about a cycle of
church life and death in which he saw the church as growing
from a sect status to a denominational stage.[9] But Towns' elabo-
ration of the Troeltsch-Moberg cycle is worth our consideration.

Elmer Towns sees the church as beginning as a fundamentalist

sect, complexifying to the stage of institution, developing further
to the point of being a full-fledged denomination, and then dete-
riorating and dying.[10] There might be some question raised that
Towns' research is too partial to be conclusive. "Which denominations are fully dead?" one might ask. Even Shakers, the asex-
ual, pro-celibacy, colonizing bean-bakers still have a few members left alive. Like whooping cranes, they are hard to count:
sometimes there are thirty Shakers, sometimes twenty-seven—
but they are not completely dead. The other denominations
which appear to be at the last stop on the cycle of death are
still quite alive and even much stronger than the Shakers.

But let us consider Dean M. Kelley's research for a moment.
Most denominations in America grew from colonial times until
1967, when they began experiencing losses in membership. Between the years 1967 and 1970, the largest Lutheran churches
in America lost 200,000 members; and their Sunday Schools
were reduced by nearly 15 percent. The Episcopalians during
those same years lost over 100,000 church members and 250,000
Sunday School members. During those same years the Method-
ists lost in excess of 300,000 members in church and a staggering
2,000,000 in Sunday School. Even the formidable Roman
Catholic Church showed a slight decrease in 1970.. And so the
same general trend holds in all other major denominations with
the exception of Missouri Synod Lutherans and Southern Baptists. The former continued showing slight increases while the
latter grew at the rate of 2.26 percent per year.[11]

Dean Kelley lists the traits of a strong religion:

1. Commitment—a willingness to sacrifice status possessions,
   safety or life itself for the cause of the company of the
   faithful. . . . a total response to total demand. . . . a total
   identification of the individual's goals with the group's.
2. Discipline—a willingness to follow leadership without
   question and a willingness to suffer sanctions for infraction
   rather than leave the group.
3. Missionary zeal—an eagerness to tell the "goodness" and

a refusal to be silenced . . . the use of a stylized and cryptic (an evangelical) language.

4. Absolutism—a belief that we have the truth and that all others are in error. A closed system of meaning and value which explains everything.
5. Conformity—an intolerance of dissent and a strong tendency toward separatism.
6. Communication—all talk and no listen. . . . keep yourself unspotted from the world and preach for converts but do not listen to compromising logic.[12]

I believe Kelley is right in the accounting of these characteristics. However, there is a list of more positive traits that he has missed.

The "fundamentalist sect" is often characterized by enthusiasm. There is often an obvious warmth at work in the conservative evangelical fellowship. Their friendliness is almost threatening to the shy person. Rigidity is replaced by high flexibility. Concern for ritual is usually replaced by a high concern for the individual.

Both Kelley and Towns agree that it is in the fundamentalist sect that religion is possessed by the best life signs. If we are prone to put down the fundamentalist sect stage of church growth, we need to remember that Southern Baptists themselves were there not so very many years ago and that we, ourselves, are also progressing further around the wheel of complexity and death, according to Towns.

Dean Kelley also feels that our own rate of growth is slowing and that we will also begin to show a decline in membership in the years ahead. Towns' comment is that Southern Baptists are to be found at each stage of the sociological cycle. Some are at the fundamentalist sect stage; others are already at the deterioration stage and stiff with complexity. He goes on:

In reference to the sociological cycle, Southern Baptists do not usually classify themselves by the level *fundamentalist* and *evangelical.* Rather they tend to use the label *conservative* and *liberal,* leaving out the mid-point designation of evangelicalism or institutionalizationism.[13]

In his book *The Secular City,* Harvey Cox discussed the bankruptcy of American denominationalism.[14] Cox suggested that we proceed on to a religionless Christianity. If we really are mature, of course, it is the "Bonhoefferish" thing to do.

As a pastor I reject Cox's solution. While I cannot return to the fundamentalist sect position as a mentality, I believe that I can return to that position as a platform for preaching the gospel. From the vantage point of the new evangelicalism, I can view man as a spiritual being. From that elevation I can see that man without Christ is both spiritually and sociologically desperate.

I cannot tell you exactly where *I* am on the sociological cycle. While I do not carry my Thompson Chain Reference Bible to concert halls or football games, I always carry a New Testament to be completely usable to the Spirit. I have faced the absurdity of Andy Warhol; but I know of Watchman Nee, too. I have followed C. S. Lewis to "Perelandra" and Stanley Kubric to "2001." I have taught literacy to a carpenter and existentialism at the Free University. I have cried for agnostics I could not answer and rejoiced with seekers whom I overanswered. To some men in boldness, I have said too much. To others in sheer cowardice, I have said nothing.

But I have yet to meet my first man whose greatest need was not spiritual. And in fifteen years of trying to grow churches for Christ and the Home Mission Board, my appetite for souls is often voracious. Sometimes I feel that my sociology is lopsided, that I might be happier if I would paint a poster for the Right-to-Lifers or join Nader's Raiders. Once or twice I really wanted to paint a placard for the M. I. A. campaign; but by the time I got back from soul-winning visitation, it was too late to stop and pick up the tempera.

I don't always feel culturally respectable having arrived at middle age as a "Jesus freak," a "gospel gadfly," tearing around the suburban scene with my testimony and spiritual propositions. But I have a fond hope that someday I may get to hear these delightful words from the *Exaggerated Paraphrase:* "Well done, thou good and faithful servant,/ Thou hadst a good Sociology. . . ./ You saw every man clearly. . . . one at a time."

Notes

1. Urban T. Holmes III, *The Future Shape of Ministry* (New York: Seabury Press, 1971), p. 144.

2. David L. Mueller, *Karl Barth* (Waco: Word Books, 1972), p. 99.

3. Ibid., p. 109.

4. Holmes, p. 191.

5. Ibid., pp. 191–192.

6. Sherwood Eliot Wirt, *The Social Conscience of the Evangelical* (New York: Harper & Row, 1968), pp. 40–41.

7. John Bisagno, *How to Build an Evangelistic Church* (Nashville: Broadman Press, 1971), p. 67.

8. Ibid., pp. 159–160.

9. Ibid.

10. Ibid., p. 156.

11. Dean M. Kelley, *Why Conservative Churches Are Growing* (New York: Harper & Row, 1972), pp. 1–21.

12. Ibid. pp. 58–79.

13. Elmer L. Towns, *America's Fastest Growing Churches* (Nashville: Impact Books, 1972), p. 156.

14. Harvey Cox, *The Secular City* (New York: The Macmillan Company, 1966).